SCIENCE
EXPERIMENTS
TO BLOW YOUR MIND

ARCTURUS

This edition published in 2015 by Arcturus Publishing Limited
26/27 Bickels Yard, 151–153 Bermondsey Street,
London SE1 3HA

Copyright © Arcturus Holdings Limited

Author: Thomas Canavan
Editors: Joe Harris and Rebecca Clunes
Designer: Elaine Wilkinson
Illustrator: Adam Linley
Experiments Co-ordinator: Anna Middleton
Step photography: Thomas Middleton
All other photographs by Shutterstock

ISBN: 978-1-78599-098-4
CH004773US
Supplier: 26, Date 1215, Print run 4492

Printed in China

SCIENCE
EXPERIMENTS
TO BLOW YOUR MIND

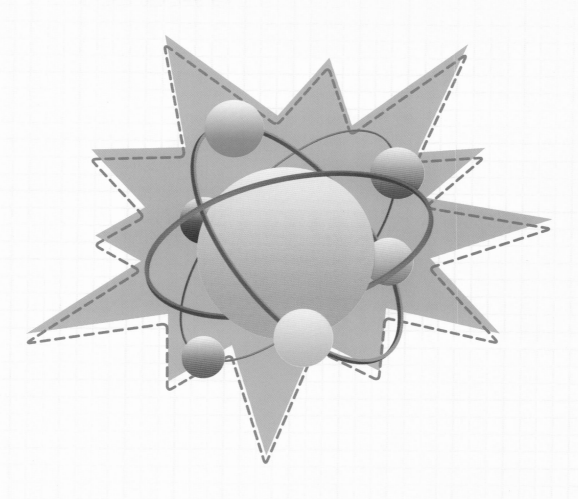

ARCTURUS

Contents

4

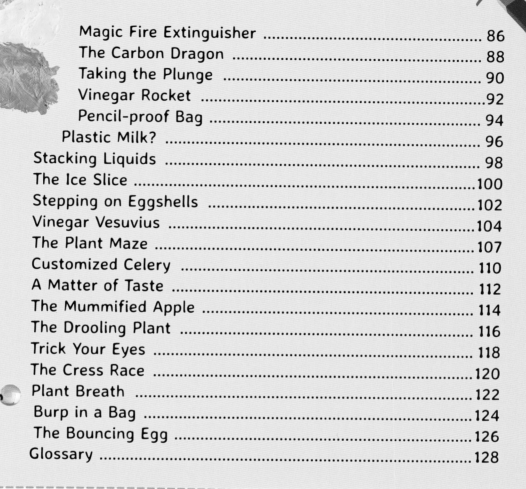

Having Fun and Being Safe

Inside this book you'll find a whole range of exciting science experiments that can be performed safely at home. Nearly all the equipment you need will be found around your own house. Anything that you don't have at home should be available at a local store.

We have given some recommendations in the "Top Tips" sections to let you know when adult help might be needed. However, the degree of adult supervision will vary depending on the age of the child and the experiment. We would recommend close adult supervision for any experiment involving cooking equipment, sharp implements, electrical equipment, or batteries.

The author and publisher cannot take responsibility for any injury, damage, or mess that might occur as a result of attempting the experiments in this book. Always tell an adult before you perform any experiments, and follow the instructions carefully.

The No-spill Glass

So much of what seems like pure magic can be traced to basic scientific principles. And that's why some of the best experiments can be presented as if they were tricks. You'll get oohs and aahs if you perform this one in front of an audience. And why not? You seem to be defying gravity!

YOU WILL NEED

- Drinking glass (glass works better than plastic)
- Water
- Orange juice
- A piece of thin cardboard that's bigger than the mouth of the glass
- A sink or basin

1

Add some orange juice to the glass and then add water to about two-thirds full.

2

Rest the glass on a counter or table and place the cardboard on it. Make sure that the cardboard extends beyond the rim of the glass all around.

3

Hold the glass, right-side up, with one hand and press the cardboard down on it with the other.

4

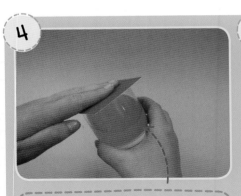

Keeping your hand pressed firmly to the cardboard, quickly turn the glass over so that it's upside-down.

5

Hold the glass in front of you, upside-down, with both hands still in place. This will assure your audience that the liquid is still there, waiting to spill.

6

Keep hold of the glass but remove your other hand from the cardboard. It should remain in place, with no water spilling out!

HOW DOES iT WORK?

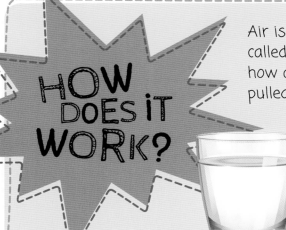

Air is pressing on us all the time, from all directions. It's called air pressure. By flipping the glass, you changed how air was pushing on the water. The force of gravity pulled the water down, and the air inside the glass filled in some of the space that the water left behind. The same amount of air now took up more space—and that meant that its pressure got smaller. There was less air pressure pushing down on the water than pushing up on the cardboard... so the water in the glass stayed put!

TOP TiPS!

This experiment is very reliable... but just in case, perform it over a sink or basin.

WHAT HAPPENS IF...?

If you have enough time—and your sink is big enough—you could try the experiment with glasses filled with different liquids and cardboard of different sizes. You could also see if there's an upper limit to the amount of "oomph" that the air pressure can give.

REAL LiFE SCIENCE

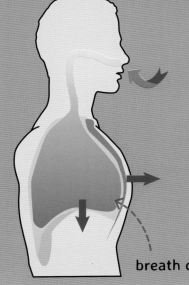

You're using the air pressure around you every time you take a breath. The diaphragm, a muscle in your lower chest, contracts (gets smaller), making more space in your chest. That extra space in your chest lowers the pressure of the air inside... and the air outside (still at normal pressure) rushes in.

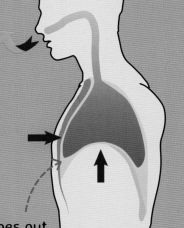

breath comes in

breath goes out

The Balancing Forks

How good is your sense of balance? This experiment uses a little bit of science to pull off a trick that looks like magic. The forks seem to be floating in mid-air, but in fact they are just balanced—really well!

YOU WILL NEED

- 2 identical metal forks
- 2 toothpicks
- Sturdy salt shaker

1

Stick one of the toothpicks into a hole in the salt shaker so that it stands upright, like a flagpole. Hold the forks upright with their curved tines pointing at each other.

2

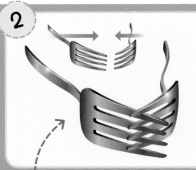

Push and "weave" the forks together so that their tines overlap. They should form an "x" shape, which you can balance on your finger beneath the crossed tines.

3

Feed the other toothpick through the first gap of the underside of the tines, through to the back, and through the first gap of the other fork.

4

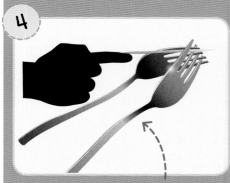

You should be able to balance the arrangement on the end of your finger.

5

Carefully place the point of the second toothpick on the top point of the first toothpick. Remove your hand and the entire arrangement will balance on the two meeting points. It looks impossible!

HOW DOES IT WORK?

Of course, this wonderful display is not as impossible as it looks. It relies on something called the center of mass. That term refers to the "middle point" of an object, or collection of objects—so there's an equal amount of mass on either side.

Here the center of mass is at the end of the toothpick that was stuck into the forks. Equal amounts of mass press in on it from all sides, keeping it secure. Even the force of gravity is "funneled" into this point, which is why people sometimes refer to the "center of gravity."

REAL LIFE SCIENCE

Have you ever seen tightrope walkers as they make their way between skyscrapers or across deep canyons? Most of them use a long pole, jutting far to each side of them, as they find each step. The pole helps to keep the mass of the tightrope walker over the center of gravity—where their feet meet the cable—just as the long fork handles focus the center of gravity on the toothpick.

TOP TIPS!

It's easier to press the forks on a counter as you weave them together.

WHAT HAPPENS IF...?

Arrange about eight playing cards along the floor of a hallway, making a zigzag of "stepping stones" about 20 inches (50 cm) apart. Try walking along this path, only stepping on the cards. Now try it again, holding a broom handle for balance. Is it easier? Faster?

Waterproof Paper

Here's another science demonstration that you can present to your friends as a trick... or even a little drama. Imagine that you've got to hide an important letter and enemy soldiers have burst in while you're washing glasses. How can you keep it hidden, and dry?

1

Run water into the sink or basin until it's about two-thirds full.

2

Hold up the paper and tell your friends it's the document.

3
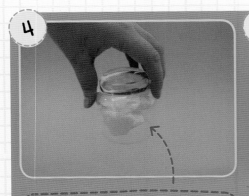
Scrunch up the paper and push it to the bottom of the glass.

4

Tip the glass upside-down to make sure the paper is lodged in and won't fall out. If it falls, scrunch it up a bit more loosely so it will fit in better.

5

Now plunge the glass, upside-down, into the water until it's completely underwater. This is the bit where you're hiding the "document."

6
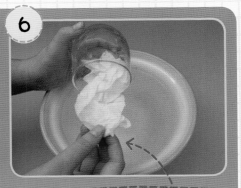
The soldiers have gone to look somewhere else for the document. It's safe to take the glass out of the water. Take the paper from the glass. It's still dry!

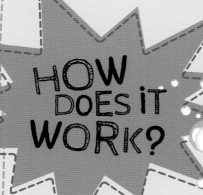

HOW DOES IT WORK?

If you looked closely at the sink or basin as you pushed the glass down, you'll have seen the water level rise a little. That rise comes from the water that was displaced (pushed out of the way). And it's the air in the glass that's doing the pushing. Air would normally rise up through water in bubbles, but the upturned glass blocks it. Since the air isn't going to go down, it stays lodged inside the glass. That lodged air forms a barrier against the water, so the paper stays dry.

REAL LIFE SCIENCE

Water displacement lies at the heart of many scientific and engineering activities. One of the most important is the study of buoyancy, how and why things float (or don't). It's all about how much water they displace. If a ship or submarine weighs less (because it contains lots of air) than the water it would displace, then it floats. Submarines can control their buoyancy by filling tanks with water to make them sink, or filling those tanks with air to rise again.

WHAT HAPPENS IF...?

Float a plastic toy in a measuring jug that's half full of water and sitting in the sink. Now take a glass that's narrower than the jug, turn it upside-down and press it down on the water around the toy. The toy goes down to the bottom! That's because the air trapped in the glass is pushing it down.

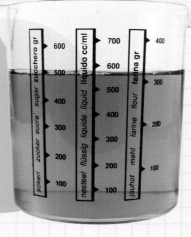

The Last Straw

You've just had a long bike ride and you've come home thirsty. Look! Someone's made a cool drink for you, complete with a straw. Ahhh, just what you need, so you take the straw in your mouth, begin to suck, and... nothing! What's going on?

1

Ask an adult to make a hole in the center of the lid, using a hammer and nail.

2

See whether the straw fits through the hole. If not, ask the adult to widen the hole by working the nail around it a bit.

3

Feed the straw through the lid so that it will almost reach the bottom of the jar when the lid goes back on.

4
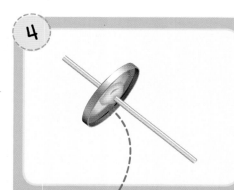
Put some poster putty around the straw where it meets the lid. This will make it airtight.

5

Fill the jar about three-quarters of the way with a drink and screw the lid back on tightly. Try sucking it....

6

... but you'll find that it's impossible!

12

HOW DOES IT WORK?

Sucking through a straw isn't so much about pulling (sucking) as it is about pushing. Air does the pushing, through the force known as air pressure. Normally when you suck through a straw, you suck in—which reduces the pressure inside your mouth. But the air all around the drink is pushing down on the top of the liquid in the glass. That pressure is greater than the (reduced) pressure in your mouth, so the drink gets pushed along. But if you cover the drink completely, that outside air can't reach the liquid to push down on it… so you can't get any drink.

REAL LIFE SCIENCE

You can see the effects of changing air pressure every day, just by looking out the window. The Earth's spinning, teamed up with other factors such as the difference in temperature over land and over the ocean, affects air pressure. When areas of high pressure and low pressure meet, we get winds and other weather effects.

WHAT HAPPENS IF...?

You can try this trick the opposite way around. Stick a straw in the mouth of a half-full bottle of water and seal it with modeling clay. Now blow hard into the straw and then stand back. As soon as you stop blowing, water comes rushing out of the straw. Your blowing increased the pressure of the air inside the bottle so that it was more than the air pressure outside.

Tabletop Catapult

Towering catapults were some of the most fearsome weapons in the Middle Ages. They could hurl huge stones, burning bales of hay and even manure over castle walls. You can harness science to create your own kitchen catapult, although your "ammo" will be ping-pong balls.

1

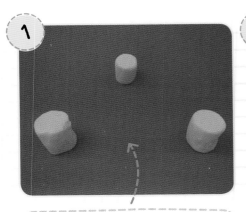

Lay three marshmallows on a table to form a triangle with three equal sides.

2

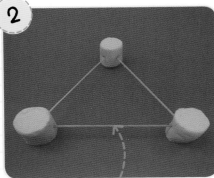

Use three skewers to connect the marshmallow triangle.

3

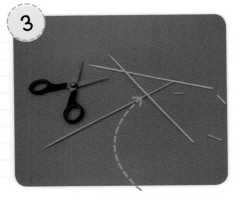

Cut ¾ inch (2 cm) off three more skewers.

4

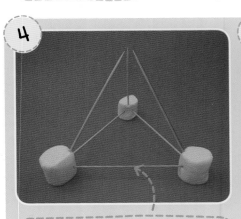
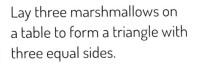

Stick these three skewers into the top of the marshmallows, pointing upward and toward each other to form a pyramid.

5

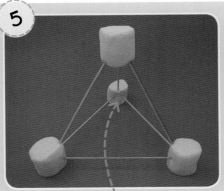

Stick a marshmallow on the top of those three skewers, giving the pyramid a top.

6

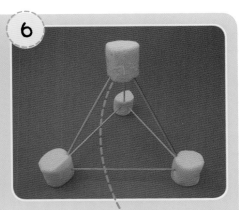

Wrap a few layers of tape around this top marshmallow.

14

7

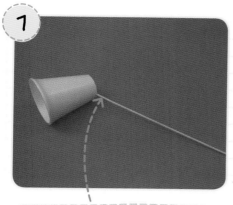

Stick another skewer at an angle through the paper cup. It should come in through the side of the cup, but near the bottom.

8

Put a little poster putty around the inside and outside of the cup, where the skewer has just entered.

9

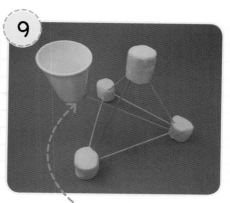

Stick the other (non-cup) end of that skewer into one of the marshmallows that form the base.

10

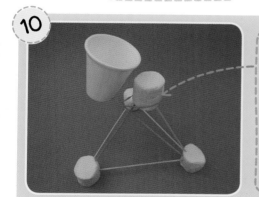

Place one end of a rubber band around the "cup" end of the skewer and the other end of the band around the top marshallow. The paper cup will be next to that top marshmallow.

11

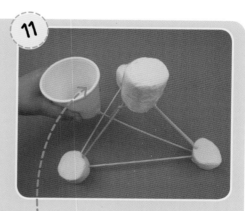

Put a ping-pong ball into the paper cup and pull down on the cup, stretching the rubber band.

Let go of the cup... and send the ball flying!

12

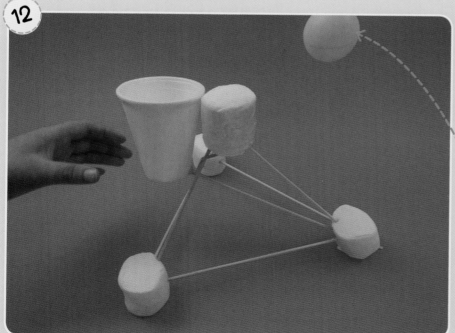

Continued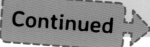

HOW DOES IT WORK?

There are some important scientific principles at work here. First of all, the catapult itself is an example of a machine known as a lever. The base marshmallow (the other end from the cup) is known as the fulcrum. As you pull back on the cup you build potential energy. This becomes kinetic (motion) energy when you release your fingers and the cup flies up. When the cup stops, the ball flies off because of Newton's First Law of Motion—an object in motion wants to stay in motion. It's very similar to a simple slingshot.

TOP TIPS!

Be careful where you aim your catapult. Make sure the ball won't hit something valuable.

WHAT HAPPENS IF...?

If you built a catapult with a longer arm, the ball would go farther. That's because the tip of the arm would move farther in the same time that the fulcrum end moved the same distance. Traveling farther in the same time means going faster—and giving the load more force. Think of how much farther you could cast with a long fishing rod compared to a short stick.

REAL LIFE SCIENCE

Some of the catapults that armies used in the Middle Ages were huge. They would be assembled near a castle and then wheeled into range. It was common for catapults to send huge rocks up to 220 pounds (100 kg) more than 1,000 feet (300 m) into—or over—castle walls.

Ping-Pong Launcher

Isn't it great when you have a scientific explanation to avoid getting into trouble? How's this one? "Dad, the reason that ping-pong ball bounced off your nose while you were reading the paper was that I was demonstrating kinetic energy."

YOU WILL NEED

- Cardboard postal tube, about 2 inches (5 cm) in diameter
- 2 empty paper towel tubes
- Packing tape
- 2 long rubber bands
- Ping-pong ball
- A hole puncher
- String
- Scissors
- Ruler

1

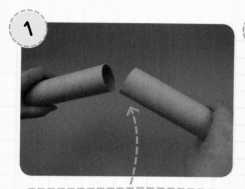

Push one paper-towel tube about 1 inch (2.5 cm) inside the other.

2

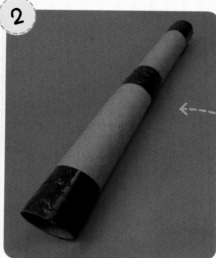

Tape around the join between the tubes and tape around (but not over) the end of the tube pair.

3

Use the hole puncher to make two holes near one end of the tube pair. The holes should be on opposite sides of the tube, about 1 inch (2.5 cm) from the end.

4

Use the same technique to make two holes in the postal tube.

5

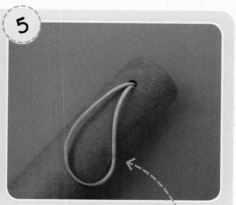

Feed a rubber band a little way through one of the holes in the postal tube.

17

6

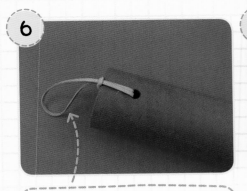

Feed the other end of the same band through the rubber-band loop inside the tube and give it a tug to tighten it in place.

7

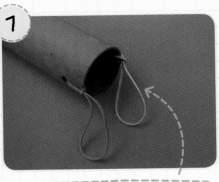

Take the second rubber band and secure it through the other hole in the postal tube in the same way.

8

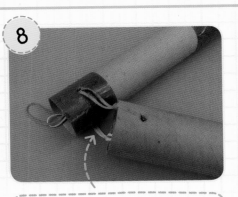

Feed each of the rubber bands through a hole in the cardboard tube pair.

9

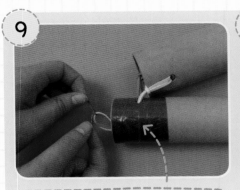

Cut a 2-3 inch (5-7 cm) piece of string and use it to tie the ends of the rubber bands together.

10

Pull the cardboard tube gently from the postal tube so the tied bands nestle inside the cardboard tube. Then tape over that end of the tube.

11

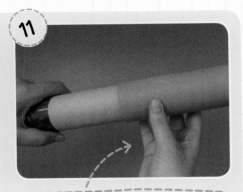

Feed the other end of the cardboard tube into the postal tube. Pull it gently when it juts from the end of the postal tube, so that the "band" end is pulled inside.

12

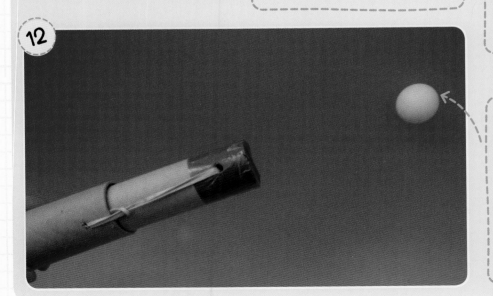

Drop a ping-pong ball into the open end of the postal tube and pull back on the jutting cardboard tube... until you let go and...

FIRE!

HOW DOES IT WORK?

This experiment is all about—remember this when you need an excuse—types of energy. As you pulled back on the cardboard tube, you were building up potential energy. That's the type of energy that's ready to be used in another form. Then, when you let go and one tube went rushing through the other tube (with the ball along for the ride), the potential energy was transformed into kinetic energy. That's the scientific term for the energy of movement. In this case it was enough to send the ball flying.

TOP TIPS!

- If the postal tube is too thick for the hole punch, you could ask an adult to make the holes with a nail and hammer.

- Don't aim your catapult at a person (not even your dad reading the paper!).

WHAT HAPPENS IF...?

... you did the same experiment with much bigger tubes, about 10 feet (3 m) long, and much longer rubber bands? You guessed it: the ball would go flying that much farther and faster. That's because the potential energy would be that much greater—and it would turn into much greater kinetic energy at the release.

REAL LIFE SCIENCE

Have you ever seen, or ridden on, a roller coaster? It packs a real thrill by its constant transformation of potential and kinetic energy. Climbing up those hills ever... so... slowly... builds up enormous energy. This gets transformed into kinetic energy as soon as it rushes down the other side.

Hey—No Pressure!

Just how hard it is it to blow a couple of balloons apart? Pretty easy, you'd think... unless science stands in your way. You'll huff and you'll puff, but you'll wind up wound up and winded unless you read up on just what's happening. Clue: it's about pressure.

YOU WILL NEED

- 2 balloons
- 2 high-backed chairs
- String
- Scissors
- Ruler
- Water from a faucet
- Empty paper-towel roll
- A broom

1
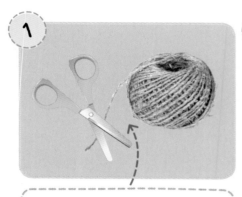
Cut two lengths of string, each about 20 inches (50 cm) long.

2

Run some cold water slowly and pour some (about a finger's width high) into each balloon. Blow them up and tie them.

3
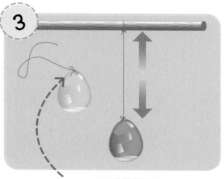
Tie a string to each balloon and tie the other end of each string loosely around the broom handle.

4
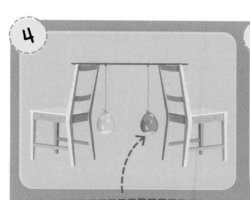
Arrange the chairs so they're facing away from each other and rest the broom handle across so that the balloons hang down.

5
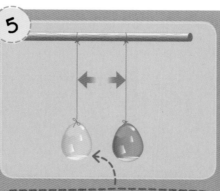
Slide the balloons so that they're about 4 inches (10 cm) apart. The water inside them keeps them steady.

6
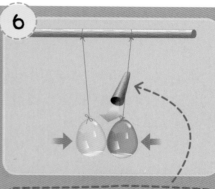
Crouch or kneel to the level of the balloons, hold the tube to your mouth and blow hard between the balloons. Instead of being driven apart, they're drawn together!

20

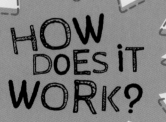

HOW DOES IT WORK?

You're supplying the force (your breath) to speed up a channel of air. And when air—or any other gas or liquid—begins to move faster, it loses pressure. Remember that air pressure is all around us, pushing in with a force of 14.7 pounds for every square inch (1 kg per square cm).

That force remains the same for all of the air surrounding the balloons, except for the fast-moving channel that you've created. That faster-moving air has less pressure, meaning it doesn't push so hard against the balloons. And that's why they get pushed together.

REAL LIFE SCIENCE

Engineers and architects need to understand the effects of varied air pressure on individual skyscrapers and groups of them. Sudden or extreme drops of pressure can put stress on those buildings, and it's important to have precautions built into them.

WHAT HAPPENS IF...?

Poke a hole through the bottom of a paper cup and stick a drinking straw through, plugging up any gaps with modeling clay. Rest an inflated balloon on the cup and blow through the straw. As long as you're blowing, the balloon will remain attached to the cup, even if you tilt the cup down. It's that air pressure again.

the Sword in the...Rice

Legend says that only Arthur, the true king of Britain, could pull a sword from a stone. But how did the sword become stuck, and could you create something similar? If you can pull this "sword" out, maybe you have a royal ancestor somewhere in your family tree...

1
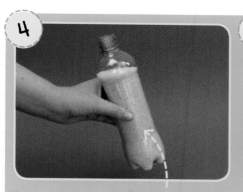
Pour rice into the bottle, filling it about halfway.

2
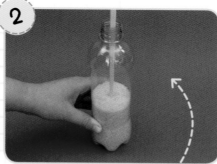
Hold the bottle steady and push the skewer straight down through the opening into the rice.

3
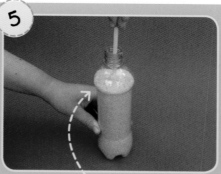
Without holding the bottle, slowly pull the skewer upward—it should come out of the rice easily.

4

Fill the bottle almost to the top with more rice and tap the bottle several times on the table.

5
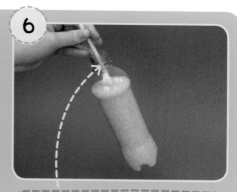
Push the skewer down through the rice again.

6

Pull up on the skewer again—this time you should be able to pick up the whole bottle.

22

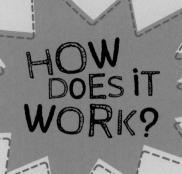

HOW DOES IT WORK?

This demonstration relies on friction, the force that resists the motion of moving objects. You come across friction when you use the brakes on your bike, or push a box along a carpet, or when you rub your hands together to warm up.

There's also friction between the grains of rice. The first skewer pulled out easily because there wasn't much friction. But the second time you had more mass (the bottle had more rice) and by tapping the bottle you caused the grains to settle together... increasing the friction "grip" on the skewer.

WHAT HAPPENS IF...?

You can also "lock" two books together with friction. Face them together and fan the pages of both books so they overlap into the opposite book. Then try to pull them apart.

REAL LIFE SCIENCE

Engineers are always looking for ways to reduce friction, so that machinery can move more freely and vehicles can use less fuel. Oil and other lubricants reduce friction between the moving parts of machines such as car engines. The streamlined design of aircraft and racing cars reduces air resistance, which is a type of friction.

Go with the Flow

YOU WILL NEED

- Blow-dryer
- Ping-pong ball
- Empty kitchen-towel roll

Who'd have thought that a blow-dryer, a ping-pong ball, and an empty kitchen-towel roll would become pieces of scientific equipment? But it's true, and the pay-off is amazing. Prepare to get "blown away."

1

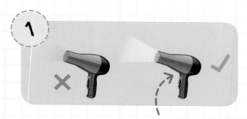

Turn the blow-dryer on using the "cool" setting. You don't need heat for the experiment. Have the ball and kitchen-towel roll close enough to pick up easily.

Hold the dryer in one hand, pointing up, and bring the ball close to it with your other hand. Hold the ball in the middle of the moving air, about 16 inches (40 cm) above the blow-dryer.

Let go of the ball. It should stay suspended in the air.

2

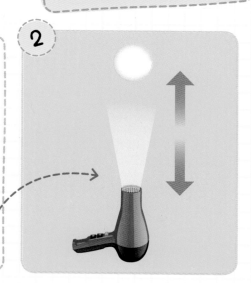

3

Tilt the dryer slowly and steadily in one direction. The ball will remain suspended even though it's no longer above the dryer.

Return the dryer to the upright position and move the paper roll in a sweeping motion so that it comes down slowly above the hovering ball. The ball will shoot up through the tube.

4

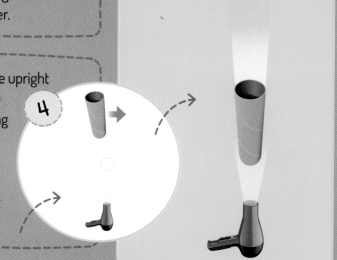

24

HOW DOES IT WORK?

This experiment is a great demonstration of Bernoulli's Principle. Daniel Bernoulli, a Swiss scientist, said that as a fluid (or gas) moves faster, its pressure decreases. Air rushing from a blow-dryer is moving faster than the surrounding air, so its pressure is less than the still air. That still air—with its stronger pressure—presses in to keep the ball inside the low-pressure moving tunnel. And when the air in that tunnel gets funneled into the narrow tube it travels faster... and its pressure gets even lower. Low enough to suck the ball into it.

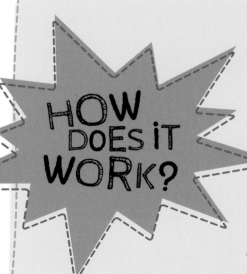

TOP TIPS!

Make sure you unplug the blow-dryer when you are finished with this experiment.

REAL LIFE SCIENCE

The Bernoulli Principle is part of the explanation of how aircraft can fly. A plane's wing is slightly curved on top but flat along the bottom. The air needs to travel faster across the top (because there's more distance to cover) than the lower air. That "top" air has a lower pressure, which means that the "bottom" air presses up.

WHAT HAPPENS IF...?

Want to try this on a bigger stage? You can do the same "hovering ball" demonstration with a leaf-blower and a beach ball. Remember: it's all about movement and pressure.

Cluck, Cluck, Cluck

It's fun when you can do a science demonstration that not only teaches people something but makes them laugh. With just a little preparation, you can create a hilarious "clucking chicken" sound effect... and learn a little about how sounds work at the same time.

YOU WILL NEED

- Light plastic cup
- String
- Sponge
- Water
- Paper clip
- Scissors
- Knife with sharp point
- Ruler

1

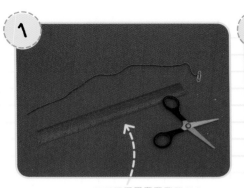

Cut a 16-inch (40-cm) length of string and tie one end around the middle of the paper clip.

2

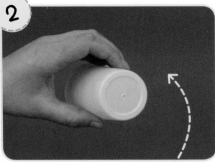

Ask an adult to use the sharp point of the knife to poke a small hole in the base of the plastic cup.

3

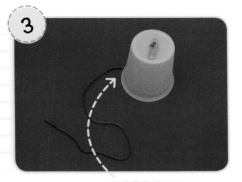

Feed the free end of the string through the hole, from the outside in. Pull it so that the paper clip acts as an anchor.

4

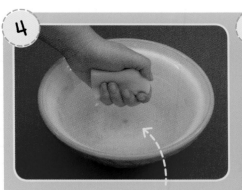
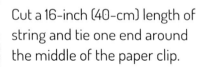

Wet the sponge and then wring it out so that it is damp but not dripping.

5

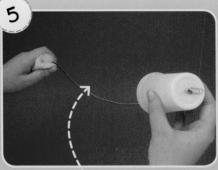

Hold the cup firmly with one hand and fold the sponge around the dangling string. Keep the sponge pinched to the string.

6

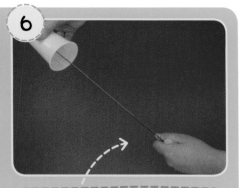

Squeeze the sponge and pull down with several sharp jerks. You should hear a loud cluck each time you pull.

HOW DOES IT WORK?

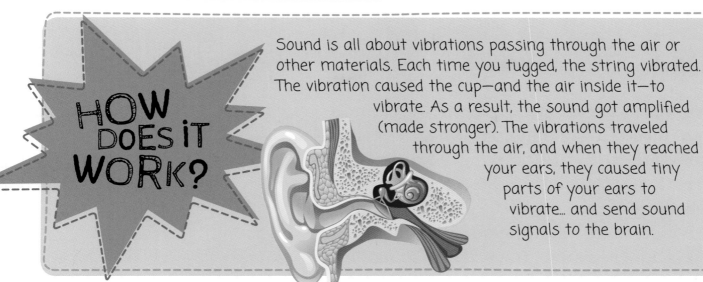

Sound is all about vibrations passing through the air or other materials. Each time you tugged, the string vibrated. The vibration caused the cup—and the air inside it—to vibrate. As a result, the sound got amplified (made stronger). The vibrations traveled through the air, and when they reached your ears, they caused tiny parts of your ears to vibrate... and send sound signals to the brain.

REAL LIFE SCIENCE

Guitars, violins, and pianos get their distinctive sound from the same combination of vibrating materials. Strings vibrate against wood (called a "sound board") to amplify the sound and give it a special rich quality.

WHAT HAPPENS IF...?

Right, so you needed the cup to produce the sound. What would happen if you tried the same experiment with a larger cup, or a smaller one? How about trying it with something made of a different material?

TOP TIPS!

Thick string or yarn work best for this experiment because they vibrate more.

The Pipes of Pan

According to ancient Greek myth, the god Pan invented the panpipes when he kissed some reeds that he had angrily broken. His breath on the reeds created a beautiful sound, recalling his sweetheart Syrinx. Panpipes still produce some haunting sounds, but you can use science—rather than myth—to make your own instrument.

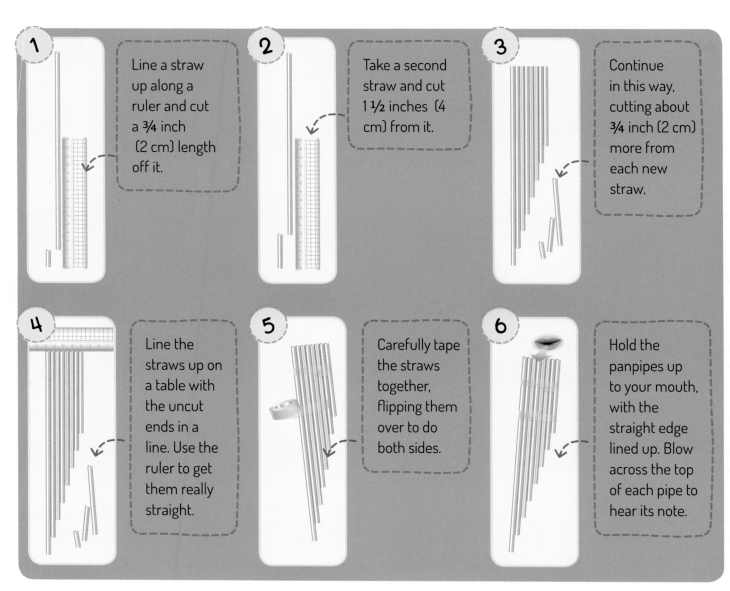

1 Line a straw up along a ruler and cut a ¾ inch (2 cm) length off it.

2 Take a second straw and cut 1 ½ inches (4 cm) from it.

3 Continue in this way, cutting about ¾ inch (2 cm) more from each new straw.

4 Line the straws up on a table with the uncut ends in a line. Use the ruler to get them really straight.

5 Carefully tape the straws together, flipping them over to do both sides.

6 Hold the panpipes up to your mouth, with the straight edge lined up. Blow across the top of each pipe to hear its note.

HOW DOES IT WORK?

This musical instrument tells you a lot about how sound works. Remember that what we recognize as sound is actually a series of vibrations passing through the air or other substances. How fast it vibrates—known as its frequency—determines whether the sound is high or low. The air passing through the shortest straw vibrates the fastest, making its "note" the highest. Each longer straw has a slightly lower frequency, making its note a little lower.

REAL LIFE SCIENCE

The pan flutes of the Inca people of South America (made of bamboo or reeds) and the mighty organs in churches and cathedrals work exactly like the instrument in this experiment. Another way to change the frequency of the sound is to change the width of the tube or pipe: a greater width produces a lower frequency.

TOP TIPS!

Both the length and the width of the straw make a difference. So you can mix and match if you can't find eight of the same size.

WHAT HAPPENS IF...?

Try the same experiment using lengths of hollow bamboo. These are often sold as garden canes. You'll need to ask an adult to cut them.

Now Hear This!

Listen up! You probably know that sound can be magnified by a megaphone or a stethoscope. But did you know that it can be magnified by... a balloon? With a little help from a gas called carbon dioxide, you can make your own super sound magnifier.

YOU WILL NEED

- Measuring cup
- Vinegar
- Teaspoon
- Funnel
- Baking soda
- Empty plastic bottle, about 1 pint (500 ml) in size
- Balloon
- Clock or wristwatch that ticks
- Sink or basin

1

Use the funnel to add 4 teaspoons of baking soda to the balloon. Set the balloon carefully to one side.

2

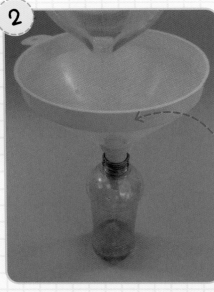

Measure out half a cup (100 ml) of vinegar with the measuring cup. Use the funnel to add it to the bottle.

3

Hold the balloon by its neck and carefully feed it over the mouth of the bottle. Slide it far enough down to hook over the lip on the top of the bottle.

4

The balloon should now be attached to the bottle with the baking soda (still dry) inside the wide part of the balloon hanging down.

30

5

Carefully raise the wide part of the balloon and hold it directly above the mouth of the bottle. The baking soda will fall into the bottle and the liquid will begin to fizz.

6

Watch as the liquid continues to fizz and the balloon above it inflates.

7

When the balloon is nearly fully inflated, pinch it and remove it from the bottle and tie it off.

8

Put the bottle in a sink or basin in case it bubbles over.

9

Place the clock on a table or counter. Make sure that there's nothing else making noise in the room.

10

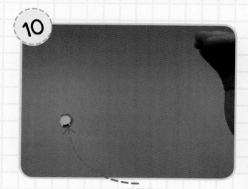

Lean down about 32 inches (80 cm) from the clock and listen to the ticks.

11

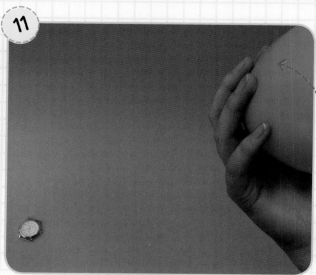

Now hold the balloon up to your ear and listen again to the ticking clock. It will sound much louder!

Continued

HOW DOES IT WORK?

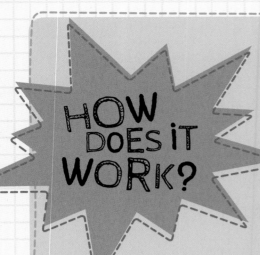

You've done two experiments in one here. The first was a chemistry demonstration—the baking soda and vinegar reacted to create salt and carbon dioxide. The carbon dioxide (known to scientists as CO_2) was the gas that filled the balloon. It is heavier than air so when sound waves (like the clock's ticks) pass through it they become bent, or refracted. It's the same principle as light waves becoming refracted as they pass through a lens. And just as a magnifying lens makes an image seem bigger, the CO_2 made the sound louder.

TOP TIPS!

When you have finished the experiment, dump the liquid mixture down the drain.

REAL LIFE SCIENCE

Sound also travels faster through a warm gas than a cooler one. This can also cause a refraction of sound waves. For example, if your friend shouted to you across a lake, you might not hear her at midday because the sound is blocked by boats in the way. At night, it is a different story. After sunset the air remains warm but the air next to a cooler surface (such as a lake) cools down. The sound waves your friend's voice makes are bent upward (traveling faster through the higher, warmer air) and then slowing down and bending downward as they pass through cooler air. The sound waves have "played leapfrog" so you can hear your friend.

WHAT HAPPENS IF...?

How would the sound change if you blew up a balloon normally and held it to your ear in this experiment? Or would it change at all? Why?

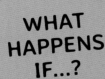

the Color Spin

You've probably heard about primary colors—red, blue, and yellow—and how artists can mix them to produce secondary colors... and all the colors of the rainbow. Here's a way for you to mix them all up without getting dirty. The result might surprise you!

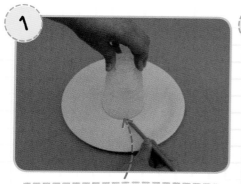

1

Turn the glass upside-down on a plate and trace a circle with the pencil.

2

Use scissors to cut the circle out.

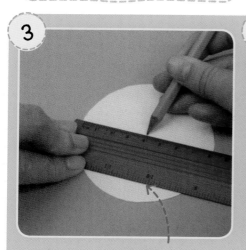

3

Measure across the widest part (the diameter) of the circle and mark the exact center with the pencil.

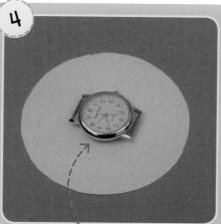

4

Lay the wristwatch on the circle so that the center of the watch is right above the center of the circle.

5

Pencil in a dot on the paper circle just outside the following watch numbers: 2, 4, 6, 8, 10, 12.

6

Remove the watch and use the ruler to draw six lines, connecting the center to the six dots and continuing to the edge. The circle should now have six identical segments.

7

Use the six markers to color in the six sections, one marker for each. Color them in this order: red, orange, yellow, green, blue, purple.

8

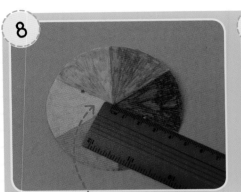

Use the ruler to mark a dot ¾ inch (2 cm) each side of the center.

9

Use the point of the scissors or the sharp point of the pencil to poke a hole through those two dots.

10

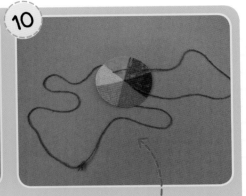

Cut a piece of string 3 feet (90 cm) long and feed it through both holes, and then tie the ends to make a loop.

11

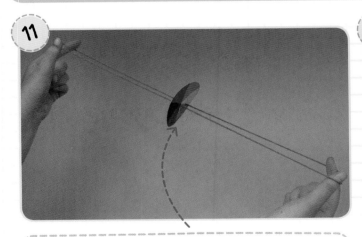

Hold the two ends of the string loop tight and slide the circle along to the middle.

12

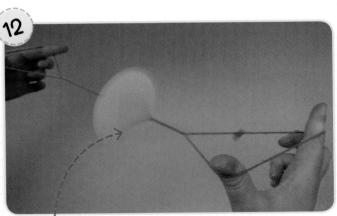

Swing the circle around the string as if you were spinning a jump rope—this will wind it up. Then pull tightly again to get it spinning. The different colors will blend, and might wind up looking white!

HOW DOES IT WORK?

This experiment tells us a lot about how colors mix and also about how our brains register colors and other images. The colors on the circle eventually spin so fast that our brains can no longer take a series of "snapshots" of them as individual colors.

Instead, the colors become mixed, and the pure mixture of all of these colors appears as white. You need to have exactly the right tone of each color for the effect to be pure white, but even the slightly darker, grayish illusion comes from the same process. In effect, you've created an artist's palette of the imagination.

TOP TIPS!

Use a longer string—and a friend holding the other end—to get a better spin.

WHAT HAPPENS IF...?

Try doing the experiment with just two of the primary colors (red, blue, and yellow). You should be able to create "secondary" colors when you spin:

red + yellow = orange
yellow + blue = green
blue + red = purple

REAL LIFE SCIENCE

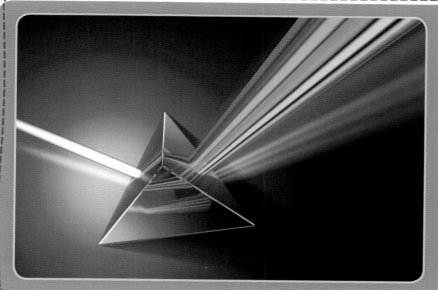

Sir Isaac Newton was the first person to try the color wheel experiment in 1672. He had noticed that when normal "white" light passed through a type of glass called a prism, it was broken up into its different colors. The color wheel shows that a rainbow of colors can be changed into white light.

Hold the Line, Please

YOU WILL NEED

- 2 plastic cups
- String, about 30 feet (9 m long)
- Paper clips
- Sharp pencil

Did you know that people had a way of talking to each other at a distance before the invention of cell phones, or even landlines? The word "line" is the clue to how they made those early telephones, and how you can make one yourself.

1

Pinch one end of the string to the tip of the pencil and gently poke it through the bottom of the cup, from the outside in.

2

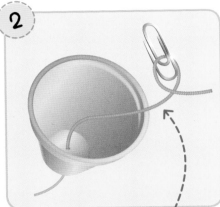

Pull the string through enough to tie it to the end of a paper clip.

3

Feed the other end of the string into the other cup and also tie it to a paper clip.

4

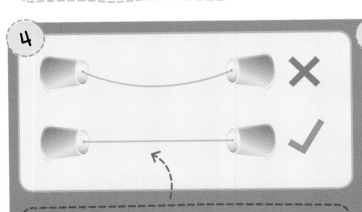

Have a friend take the other "receiver" and walk away until the string stops drooping and seems tight.

5

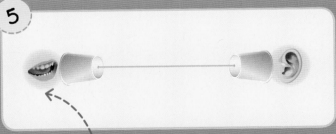

Practice speaking into one end and finding out whether your friend can hear you. Try feeding the line through the gap of an open door or behind curtains so that one of you can remain hidden.

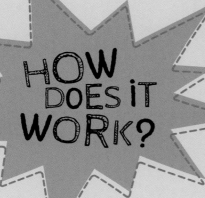

HOW DOES IT WORK?

The word telephone comes from two Greek words meaning "far" and "speak", and your homemade telephone lets you do just that. Plus it uses some of the same principles as a landline telephone.

When you speak, the string begins to vibrate, sending those vibrations down the line. The cup at the other end amplifies (increases) the sounds those vibrations make, so the other person can hear you. A normal telephone also receives and plays back vibrations, but uses electricity to send them much farther in between.

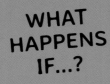

WHAT HAPPENS IF...?

This experiment is all about how sound behaves because it is a type of vibration. Try to see which type of sound vibrations travel best along your "phone line." Does it work better if you speak high (lots of vibrations) or low (not so many)?

REAL LIFE SCIENCE

This experiment works best with a short, taut string. If you try doing this experiment with a much longer piece of string, you'll notice that the other person's voice becomes harder to hear. That's because some of the vibration energy has been lost along the way, so the sound waves become weaker. Real telephone signals also lose energy over distances. That's why telephone signal boosters are needed.

What happens to the sound if the string is loose?

Cutting Light Experiment

YOU WILL NEED

- Clear glass bottle
- String
- Magnifying glass
- Metal nut, smaller than the width of the bottle's mouth
- Pencil
- A sunny day
- Scissors

This experiment is a great way to make the connection between light and heat. It does depend on sunshine, so make sure that you choose a sunny day to do it. You could even bill the experiment as a challenge you set yourself: how to cut the string without touching it.

1

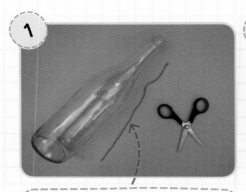

Cut a piece of string slightly shorter than the height of the bottle.

2

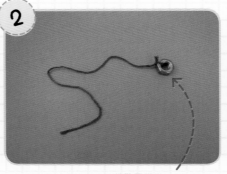

Tie the nut to one end of the string.

3

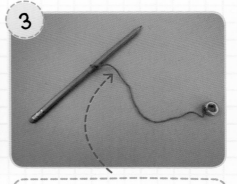

Tie the other end of the string to the middle of the pencil.

4

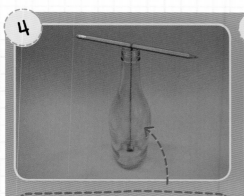

Lower the nut into the bottle almost, but not quite, to the bottom and rest the pencil across the mouth of the bottle. Wind the pencil to raise or lower the nut.

5

Use the magnifying glass to concentrate a beam of sunlight on the string. Keep the magnifying glass between the Sun and the bottle and move it until you get the brightest light shining on the string.

6

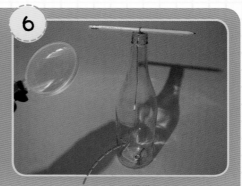

The weight of the nut pulling down will help you cut the string by burning it laser-style. The heat was concentrated on the string just as the light was.

HOW DOES IT WORK?

A magnifying glass is actually a lens, designed to change the direction of light passing through it. The magnifying glass takes the Sun's rays (which normally travel parallel to each other) and acts like a funnel to point them at a small area. Being pushed together like that makes the sunlight brighter and hotter.

That increase in temperature, focused on a small area, is enough to burn right through the string. Through the glass of the bottle? Yes, because the transparent glass absorbs very little light or heat energy from those same rays.

REAL LIFE SCIENCE

A laser is a highly technical device to focus light and to provide great heat in a small area. Lasers were once considered to be science-fiction inventions, but they're already used in surgery, engineering, and to make many products. The word laser is an abbreviation of Light Amplification by Stimulated Emission of Radiation.

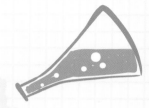

TOP TIPS!

- Never look at the Sun directly.
- Make sure that there's nothing valuable (burnable) near the bottle when you use the magnifying glass.
- Make sure an adult is present when you do this experiment.

WHAT HAPPENS IF...?

You could try the same experiment using bottles that aren't transparent. Would it work with a green bottle? How about a dark blue bottle?

The Wrong Balloon

YOU WILL NEED

- Clear balloon
- Black balloon
- Magnifying glass
- A sunny day

OK, so you can manage to blow up two balloons and have one inside the other. And you know that using a magnifying glass, you can focus sunlight to pop one of those balloons. But... it's the one inside that's just popped! Can a scientist explain that one, please?

1

Blow up the clear balloon and pinch it shut.

2

Feed the black balloon into the clear balloon, leaving some of the black balloon sticking out of the mouth of the other balloon.

3

Blow up the black balloon about halfway (it's inflating inside the clear balloon), and tie it shut.

4

Push the black balloon inside and tie the clear balloon shut. You now have two balloons, one inside the other.

5

Hold the magnifying glass so that it shines the sunlight on the pair of balloons.

6

Move the magnifying glass until it focuses the beam on the black balloon. It will pop in a few seconds.

HOW DOES IT WORK?

Darker-colored objects absorb more energy (including heat) from the light than lighter objects. And light passes through clear material with little effect. That means that it can pass through the outer (clear) balloon without bursting it. But when it reaches the inner balloon, the concentrated light (and heat) from the magnifying glass quickly heats the balloon until it pops. This also happens with other forms of radiation. X-rays pass through skin and muscle but are absorbed by bones and teeth, which is why they show up so clearly on X-ray photographs.

REAL LIFE SCIENCE

People in very hot countries often dress in light colored clothing. That's because light colors don't absorb as much heat as darker clothing would.

TOP TIPS!

- Never look directly at the Sun.

- Don't let the magnifying glass focus its light on anything delicate or valuable.

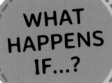

WHAT HAPPENS IF...?

Try doing the experiment in reverse, with the clear balloon blown up inside the black one. Is it still the inside balloon that pops? Why is that?

The Disappearing Coin

You've probably heard people say, "My goodness—where has all that money gone? It's just disappeared." Here's a chance to make some money really disappear, although you can also make it reappear. It's all about light. Try it as a magic trick with an audience.

1

Place a glass on a counter or table where you'll do the experiment. Fill the other glass with water.

2

Set up chairs so that the audience's eyes will be about level with the rim of the empty glass. You don't want them looking down from above.

3

Once your audience is seated, place a coin on the table and put the empty glass on top of it. Everyone should be able to see the coin through the glass.

4

Now pour about half the water from the full glass into the empty glass.

5

Ask the audience whether they can see the coin. It's disappeared!

6

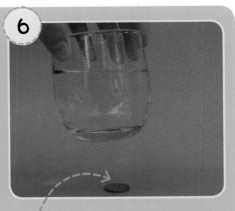

Take the glass away from the coin. It has reappeared—by magic!

HOW DOES IT WORK?

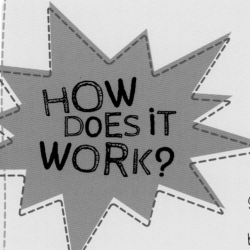

This trick is really a demonstration of the way light bends (or "refracts") as it passes through different substances. In fact, light travels "at the speed of light" only when it's going through a vacuum (which means nothing, not even air). It slows and refracts as it passes through other things.

It doesn't refract much when it passes through air, but it bends a lot more going through water. So even though you're looking straight at where the coin should be, you can't see it because the light reflected from it has gone off in a different direction.

REAL LIFE SCIENCE

Scientists and engineers use refraction in many ways. Knowing how much an ingredient (such as salt or sugar) changes a liquid's refraction is a big help. They can measure a mixture's refraction to see whether it contains too much, or too little, of such ingredients.

WHAT HAPPENS IF...?

You could try the same experiment, but this time use a glass with a bendy straw in it. If you look at the glass from the side, the straw appears to be broken.

The CD Rainbow

Maybe you know that white is actually all the colors mixed together and seen at once. And you know that you can "build" white by adding those colors together. Here's a chance to do the opposite—split white apart to reveal its hidden color ingredients.

1

If it's a sunny day, stand by a window and hold the CD in front of you. It should be shiny side up, with the printed side down. Hold the CD almost flat and observe the light reflected from it.

2

Tilt the CD a little left and right, ahead and back, until you see band of different colors.

3

See whether you can project those colors on the window frame or other blank surface near the window.

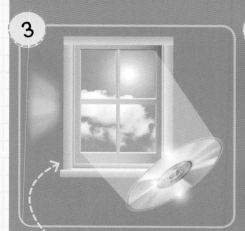

4

Go to a darker part of the room and hold the CD with one hand and the flashlight beyond it, pointing back down on the CD.

5

Tilt the flashlight and the CD until you start to see the rainbow, just as you did with the sunlight. By angling both of them, you're reflecting light from the different ridges and sending out the different reflected colors.

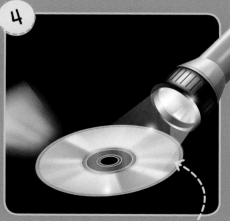

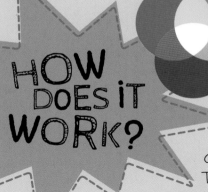

HOW DOES IT WORK?

Light, or the "white light" that we see from the Sun or a flashlight, is actually a combination of all the colors. Light travels in waves, a bit like waves approaching a beach. Sometimes ocean waves "team up" and become bigger, and sometimes they crash into each other and cancel each other out.

The shiny side of the CD is actually made of tiny ridges. Light waves reflect (bounce away) from these ridges in different angles, some "teaming up" and others canceling out. Those changes to the waves upset the neat balance of colors. Instead we see some of them more clearly.

WHAT HAPPENS IF...?

Now flip the CD over and try the same things with the shiny side down. Do you think that you'll see the rainbow of colors this time? Were your predictions right?

TOP TIPS!

Never look at the Sun directly.

REAL LIFE SCIENCE

When you see a rainbow, you're looking at a natural version of the experiment you just did. Each raindrop in the sky refracts (bends) the white light into "all the colors of the rainbow" or the spectrum. But those colors are reflected off at different angles, so we see only one of the colors from each raindrop. And with so many raindrops up there, every color gets a chance to be seen.

The Soap-Powered Boat

YOU WILL NEED

- A card about 3 x 5 inches (7 x 12 cm)
- Basin
- Water
- Scissors
- Dishwashing liquid
- Ruler
- Pencil

You probably know all sorts of ways that boats can be propelled: wind power (sails), diesel, coal and steam... but soap?! Strange as it may seem, you can build your own mini-boat and get it moving with a small dose of dishwashing liquid.

1

Use a ruler and pencil to mark the halfway point across each of the short sides of the card.

2

Use the ruler to draw two lines, each leading from one of the halfway marks down to the far corner. Then cut along the lines to create a triangle shape.

3

Mark spots about ½ inch (1.5 cm) either side of the other halfway mark and then two more marks, each one about 1 inch (2.5 cm) up from the spots you just marked.

4

Cut a rectangle out of the card by connecting those four marks. You can think of this as the space for the boat's "engine": the pointed end is its bow (front).

5

Half fill the basin with water and place your boat in one end of it, with the pointy bow facing forward. If the water is calm, the boat won't be moving.

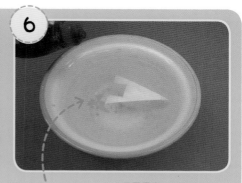

6

Carefully pour a couple of drops of dishwashing liquid into the rectangle "engine" and watch the boat move forward.

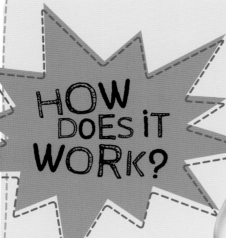

HOW DOES IT WORK?

Chemical and electrical forces hold the surface of water together, like an invisible skin, with something called surface tension. Some small objects, such as paper clips, can rest on the water's surface because of this attraction.

Adding the drops of dishwashing liquid disrupts those electrical forces, breaking the surface tension close to where the drops land. But the rest of the water isn't affected, so it still pulls in on itself. And it pulls the boat forward as it does that.

TOP TIPS!

An index card is the ideal size to make this boat.

WHAT HAPPENS IF...?

What would happen if you poured drops of dishwashing liquid on every side of the boat? Empty the basin, rinse it out thoroughly with a dishwashing sponge (to get rid of any of the earlier soap) and cut out a new boat for this attempt. Was your prediction proved right?

REAL LIFE SCIENCE

Water striders and several other types of insect use surface tension to help them walk across water without falling in. As well as using the surface tension for support, these insects have long legs pointing in different directions to spread their weight.

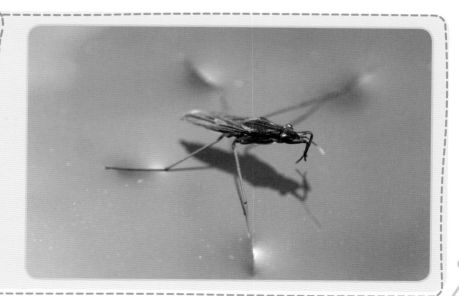

Electric U.F.O.

For years engineers have tried to design aircraft that fly silently and don't send nasty gases into the atmosphere. This experiment might set you on the way to finding the secret—you might even have a future in building flying saucers!

YOU WILL NEED

- Lightweight plastic shopping bag, about 8 inches (20 cm) across when flattened
- Balloon
- Woolen scarf or hat
- Scissors
- Pencil or crayon

1

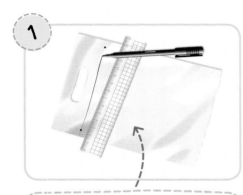

Lay the bag on a flat surface. Mark a dot on each long edge of the bag about three finger-widths down from one of the open corners.

2

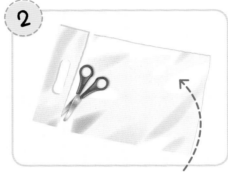

Carefully cut across the bag from dot to dot.

3

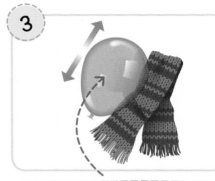

Blow up the balloon, tie it shut, then rub it briskly with the wool scarf (or hat) for about 15 seconds.

4

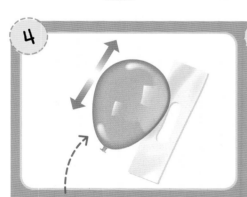

Lay the narrow plastic strip you just cut on the surface and rub it briskly with the balloon for 15 seconds.

5

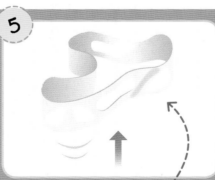

Holding the balloon in one hand, gently shake the strip so that it opens into a loop.

6

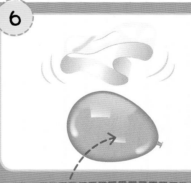

Toss the plastic loop into the air and quickly move the balloon under it. The balloon will keep it floating!

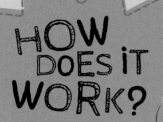

HOW DOES IT WORK?

Tiny negatively charged electrons surround the atoms of everything around us, but they can be rubbed off easily. That's what you did when you rubbed the plastic and balloon with the wool. The wool lost some of its electrons but the other materials picked them up, which gave them a negative charge.

Objects with similar charges repel (try to push away) each other, which is what the balloon and plastic ring were doing. The ring would be pulled downward by the force of gravity, but pushed back up by the action of the electrons.

REAL LIFE SCIENCE

People have been reporting Unidentified Flying Objects (UFOs) for many years. Some people think these mysterious silent aircraft come from other planets. Do they exist? And if so, how can they travel across the sky and even hover above us so silently? Maybe you have some thoughts on the subject now.

TOP TIPS!

You could try snipping your plastic ring so it has tassels. An object with many edges holds more charge.

WHAT HAPPENS IF...?

If this experiment is all about two objects rubbing together to get the same charge, what would happen if you only rubbed one of them—say, the balloon—but not the other? Make a prediction and test it yourself. How did it work?

Hold the Pepper

Imagine that you accidentally poured pepper into a half-full salt shaker. Now the salt and pepper are all mixed together and you need to get rid of the pepper. Impossible? Not if you know a little bit about the charged particles that make up all matter.

1

Pour about 2 teaspoons of salt and 2 teaspoons of pepper on to the plate.

2

Mix the salt and pepper together really well with the spoon.

3

Try to pick up some of the pepper, but no salt, using your fingers or the spoon. It's impossible!

4

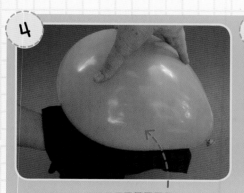

Blow up the balloon, tie it shut and rub it briskly on the sweater or scarf.

5

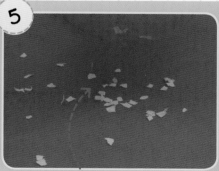

Tear off a few small (pea-sized) bits of paper and put them on the table. Hold the balloon close to them until they jump on to it. If they don't, rub the balloon some more.

6

Now lower the balloon slowly down over the plate. As you get closer you'll see grains of pepper jumping up to the balloon, leaving the salt behind.

HOW DOES IT WORK?

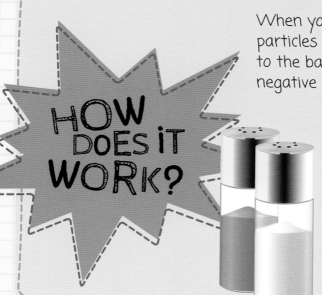

When you rubbed the balloon, some electrons (tiny particles with a negative charge) went from the wool to the balloon. The extra electrons gave the balloon a negative charge, an imbalance called static electricity.

This negative charge from the balloon pushed some of the electrons of the salt and pepper away from the balloon (remember that "opposites attract" and "likes repel"). That left more protons (tiny particles with a positive charge) facing the balloon, so the pepper jumped up. Why no salt? The same electron-proton movement takes place, but the salt is heavier so it doesn't jump up so quickly.

REAL LIFE SCIENCE

The principle of "opposite charges attracting and like charges repelling" can be put to use in many industries. MagLev (short for "magnetic levitation") trains seem to float above the track because the base of the train and the surface of the track have the same positive electric charge.

TOP TIPS!

Finely ground pepper works best for this experiment.

WHAT HAPPENS IF...?

You can do some other tricks with a charged balloon. Run a small but steady stream of water into the kitchen sink. Slowly move the balloon toward the water and it will change course. The water is attracted to the balloon just as the pepper was.

The Magic Straws

YOU WILL NEED

- 2 straight plastic drinking straws
- Plastic drinks bottle with screw-on cap
- Water
- Woolen sweater or scarf

"Straw, I command you to rotate once I wave my magic wand at you." OK, maybe that's not what a scientist would say in a lab, but you'll be able to produce some mysterious results if you harness the forces of static electricity.

1

Half-fill the bottle with water to make it more secure, and screw the cap on.

2

Rub the plastic straws briskly on the sweater or scarf for about a minute.

3

Balance one straw on the lid of the bottle.

4

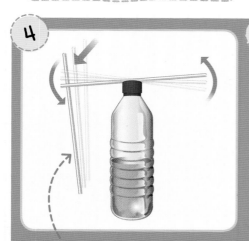

Hold the other straw and move it close to one end of the first straw, about 2 inches (5 cm) from it.

5

Move the second straw a little closer and watch the first one start to rotate. Keep the second straw about the same distance behind it. Try lifting the second straw and holding it on the other side of the resting straw. It should start to rotate the other way.

HOW DOES iT WORK?

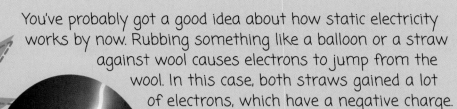

You've probably got a good idea about how static electricity works by now. Rubbing something like a balloon or a straw against wool causes electrons to jump from the wool. In this case, both straws gained a lot of electrons, which have a negative charge. And remember that "opposite charges attract and like charges repel."

So when you lowered one electron-packed (and negatively charged) straw close to another, they pushed each other away. And you got one to chase the other around and around.

WHAT HAPPENS IF...?

Instead of lowering a second straw toward the first one, use your index finger. And instead of being repelled, the straw will be attracted to your finger. Why? Because your finger has enough (positively charged) protons to attract the negatively charged electrons on the straw.

REAL LiFE SCiENCE

The whole process of "opposites attracting" and "likes repelling" lies at the heart of many industries and engineering projects. It can even help keep the skies a little cleaner. Power plants have highly (and positively) charged wires stretched across their chimneys. Tiny bits of ash and waste float past, picking up a positive charge. Just ahead lie negatively charged collection plates, which attract the ash and dirt and keep it from escaping into the outer air.

Build an Electromagnet

YOU WILL NEED

- Sharp knife
- A large iron or steel nail (not galvanized) about 3-4 inches (7-10 cm) long
- 32 inches (80 cm) of thin insulated copper wire
- A 1.5 volt battery (AAA, AA, C or D sizes all work)
- Paper clips
- Clear tape

Do you have magnets on your refrigerator? If you wanted to collect them, you could pull each one off by hand. But it might take a long time—if only you could turn off the magnetism and pick them up from the floor. This experiment shows it really is possible to build a magnet that you can turn on and off!

1

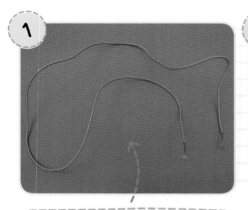

Get an adult to use the sharp knife to cut 1 inch (3 cm) of plastic coating from each end of the wire.

2

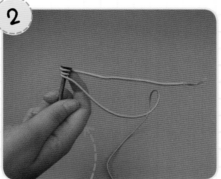

Starting around 6 inches (15 cm) from one of the stripped ends, wind the wire tightly around the nail.

3

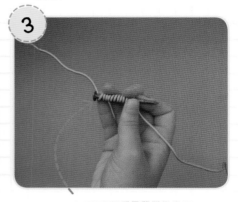

Continue wrapping the wire around the nail, taking care not to overlap the coils.

4

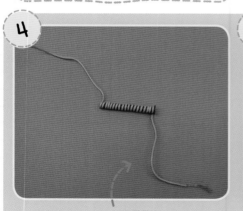

Make sure you leave at least another 6 inches (15 cm) of wire as slack at the other end.

5

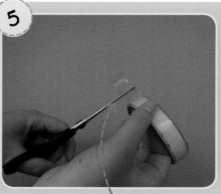

Using scissors, cut two 1 inch (3 cm) strips of tape and set them to one side.

6

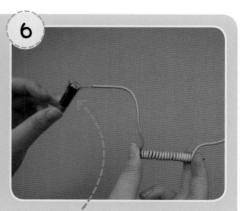

Use one piece of tape to attach one of the bare bits of wire to the underside (negative terminal) of the battery.

7

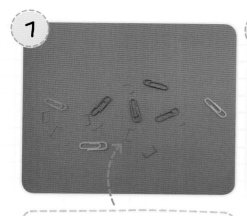

Sprinkle some paper clips and staples across a table or counter.

8

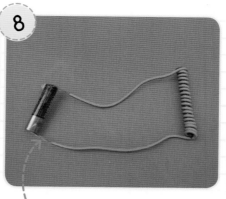

Tape the other bare bit of wire to the other (positive) side of the battery. You've now made the electromagnet.

9

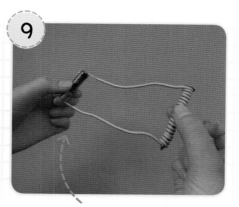

Carefully hold the combination, one hand on the middle of the battery and the other midway along the nail.

10

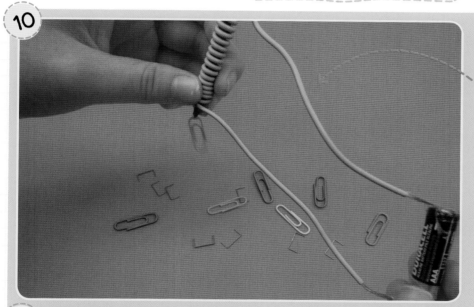

Lower the nail over the paper clips and then the staples, and see how many you can attract.

11

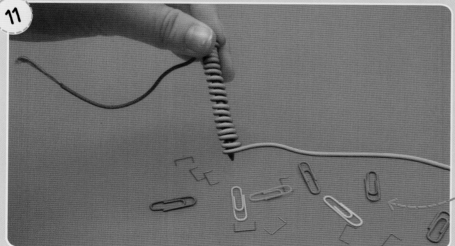

Holding the electromagnet and its dangling chain above the table, carefully remove the tape and wire from one end of the battery. The paper clips and staples will fall off.

Continued ➔

HOW DOES IT WORK?

The forces of electricity and magnetism are closely linked, which is why this is called an electromagnet. When you attached the wire to both ends of the battery, electrons began to flow through the wire from one end to the other. That flow of electrons (or current) creates a magnetic field as it passes through the wire. It rearranges the molecules of the iron in the nail so that it can attract other metal objects (like paper clips). But that flow, and the magnetic field, will stop as soon as you disconnect one end of the wire from the battery.

REAL LIFE SCIENCE

Electromagnets are all around you. They're used in all sorts of appliances, from toasters and microwave ovens to computer printers. Huge electromagnets are used in industry. In some factories, industrial lifting magnets are used to lift huge steel plates and other metallic objects.

TOP TIPS!

• Don't leave both ends of the wire connected to the battery for too long. It can get hot!

• Never use your electromagnet anywhere near an electrical outlet.

WHAT HAPPENS IF...?

Try counting the number of paper clips you can pick up when you first do the experiment. Then make a prediction about how many you will be able to pick up if you have more—or fewer—coils of wire around the nail. Test your predictions by trying it out several times.

Splitting Water

With just some simple equipment, you can produce the same process that keeps astronauts alive on the International Space Station. The secret fuel for this space-age project? Water! *Note: You will need an adult to help you with this experiment.*

YOU WILL NEED

- 2 double-ended alligator clips
- 6-volt battery
- Warm water
- 2 Number 2 pencils (without erasers)
- Clear glass jar
- Pencil sharpener
- 2 pieces of thin cardboard, large enough to cover the top of the jar
- Hole punch
- Salt
- Teaspoon

1

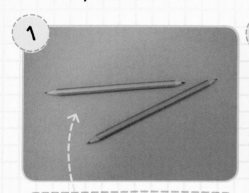

Sharpen both ends of each pencil.

2

Fill the jar nearly to the top with warm water from the faucet.

3

Add a teaspoon of salt to the water and stir.

4

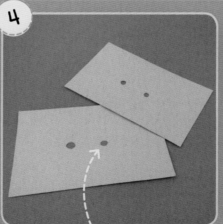

Line the pieces of cardboard up one over the other and punch two holes about 1 inch (3 cm) apart near the center.

5

Place the pair of cards on the rim of the jar and slide a pencil through each hole. The pencils should go almost to the bottom of the jar.

6

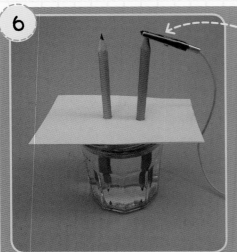

Attach a clip to the graphite ("lead") point of one pencil. Don't do anything to the clip at the other end of that lead.

Do the same with the second pencil. Each should have a clip leading from its point.

7

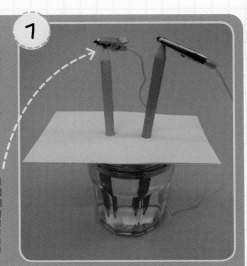

8

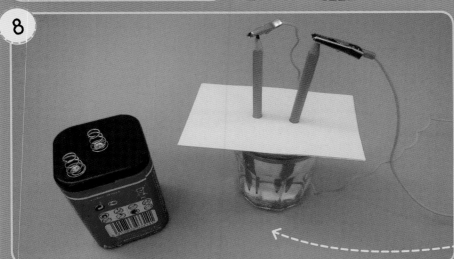

Bring the battery close to the jar/pencil arrangement.

9

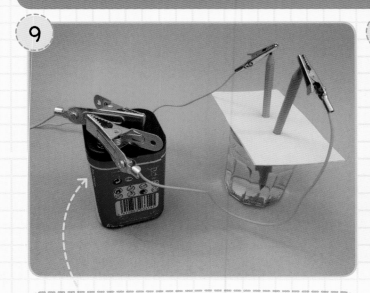

Attach each free clip to a terminal. Each lead should have one clip on a pencil and the other on a battery terminal.

10

You should start seeing bubbles emerging from the two pencil tips that are in the water.

HOW DOES IT WORK?

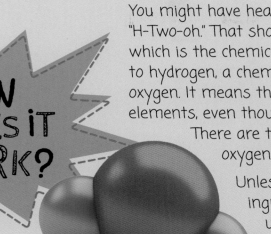

You might have heard someone refer to water as "H-Two-oh." That should really be written as "H_2O," which is the chemical formula for water. The "H" refers to hydrogen, a chemical element, and the "O" stands for oxygen. It means that water is a mixture of those two elements, even though it's not obvious to us normally. There are two hydrogen elements and one oxygen element.

Unless, of course, we break it down into its ingredients. That's what you've done here, using a process called electrolysis. The bubbles from one pencil are made of hydrogen and the bubbles from the other pencil are oxygen.

WHAT HAPPENS IF...?

It was the power of electricity that separated the hydrogen from the oxygen in the water. The salt you added was an electrolyte, which helps the water conduct electricity. Rinse out the jar and try the same experiment without adding salt. Does it still work? How is it different?

REAL LIFE SCIENCE

Oxygen is precious in many enclosed spaces. The International Space Station (ISS), which orbits the Earth, has been continuously occupied since November 2000. It uses electrolysis to generate oxygen for the astronauts on board. The electricity used in this process is generated from the ISS's solar panels.

Electro-Music

Have you ever heard grown-ups complaining, "I don't like all this new pop music. It's all electric stuff"? Well, here's a chance to "generate" a few more groans by making some electric music of your own. Your excuse if someone minds? You're just demonstrating science.

1

Tear off a strip of foil large enough to cover the top of the bowl with a little extra. Rest it on the top of the bowl.

2

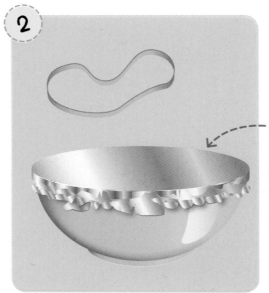

Wrap the extra bits over the edge of the bowl and secure it with the rubber band. Make the bit across the top of the bowl as tight as possible, like a drum. Tear off a much smaller strip of foil and then tear it further into pieces about the size of your thumbnail. Collect five or six of these small bits of foil.

3

Scrunch those small bits of foil into loose balls the size of small peas. Don't squeeze them too tightly, then lay them on the foil surface covering the bowl.

4

Blow up the balloon, tie it shut and then rub it vigorously back and forth across your hair for 30 seconds.

5

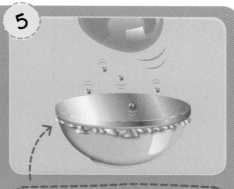

Lower and raise the balloon (with the rubbed side facing down) up and down over the bowl. Watch and listen as the foil balls jump up and fall back down on the "drum" you've made.

HOW DOES IT WORK?

This demonstration of static electricity introduces a new feature: sound. The electric power source for the experiment was your hair. Rubbing it caused lots of electrons to get attached to the balloon. That gave the "rubbed" side of the balloon a negative charge (because of the negatively charged electrons).

The positively charged protons of the metal foil were drawn to the negatively charged balloon... but only the loose bits of foil could actually jump up to it. That's because you'd attached the base to the bowl with the elastic band. And when the balls hit the flat foil they produce vibrations in the air... which we hear as sound.

WHAT HAPPENS IF...?

Here are two variations of the experiment. It's up to you to predict whether the experiment will work in the same way, differently, or not at all if you:

a. Use the same type of balloon but don't rub it first.

b. Make tightly wound foil balls that are four times as large.

REAL LIFE SCIENCE

This experiment has produced a very basic electric drum. Since the 1960s, musicians and engineers have teamed up to produce advanced electric drums. The drummer hits pads that just look like rubber, but inside are magnets that convert the "hits" into electrical signals. Those signals are sent along wires to speakers that turn them back into sounds.

Magnetic Magic

Where does science end and magic begin? One answer is "right here with this experiment." It looks like a magic trick, but it relies on some basic scientific principles. Once you've understood them, you can try on your magician's cape!

YOU WILL NEED

- Small, strong magnet, about 1 inch (3 cm) long
- String
- Scissors
- Glass jar with metal lid
- Clear tape
- Metal paper clip
- Small towel
- Trusted assistant

1

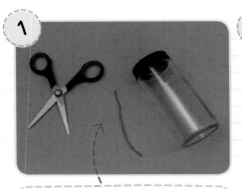

Cut a piece of string about as long as the height of the jar.

2

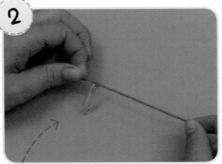

Tie the paper clip to one end of the string.

3

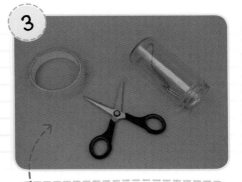

Tape the other end of the string to the inside bottom of the jar.

4

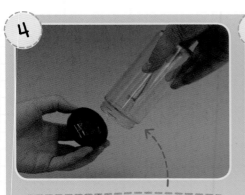

Tape the magnet to the underside of the lid and screw the lid on to the jar. Rest the jar upside-down on a table. Make sure that the clip isn't too close to the magnet at this point.

5

Hold the jar up so your audience can see the paper clip hanging down on the string.

6

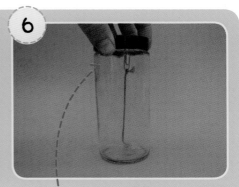

Have your assistant hold the towel in front as you carefully lay the jar down right side-up. When your assistant removes the towel, your audience will see the paper clip hanging up!

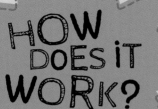

HOW DOES iT WORK?

The title tells you that magnetic force provides the drama in this experiment, or trick, or demonstration. In fact the "magical" side of the trick comes from the way that two forces are at work on the paper clip, and battling for control. The magnetic force is drawing the paper clip toward the magnet on the lid. And if the clip is close enough to the magnet (but stopped from meeting because of the string), it is stronger than the force of gravity drawing the clip toward the Earth.

WHAT HAPPENS IF...?

We know that the magnetic force passes through air— that's how this trick worked. But you can experiment to see whether it can pass through other materials. Try slipping different things (thin plastic, a sheet of paper, or other narrow objects) between the magnet and the suspended paper clip. Does the magnet still work, or does the paper clip fall?

REAL LiFE SCIENCE

Magnets and electromagnets are used in all sorts of industries to lift and move heavy or delicate objects. One of the most dramatic uses is in wrecking yards, where huge cranes lower magnets into containers. The metal contents can be easily picked up and moved around, ready for recycling.

Make Your Own Alarm

YOU WILL NEED

- A 1.5 volt battery (size AAA)
- String
- Scissors
- Poster putty
- Long paper clip
- Bulb from a 1.5 V flashlight
- A window

So you want to be a detective? Then a good way to start is to have a few tricks to see whether anyone has been where they shouldn't have gone. How can you check? By building your own intruder alarm, linked to an outside window.

1

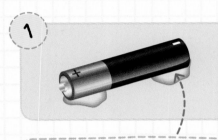

Rub a fingernail-sized blob of poster putty to a tabletop or desk and press the battery on to it securely.

2

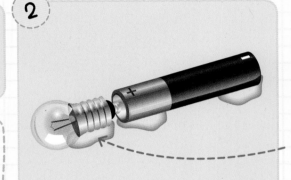

Press a smaller blob of putty just under the positive end of the battery (marked "+") and press the bulb against the battery, letting the putty hold it in place. The bulb should be on if you press it in.

3

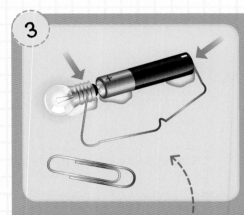

Unfold the paper clip and form a hook at one end (to pull the bulb toward the battery) and curve the other end so that it touches the negative end (marked "−") of the battery.

4

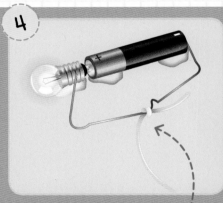

Adjust the wire and the poster putty so that the bulb is held tightly against the battery and the light stays on. Cut a piece of string long enough to reach from the battery to the handle of a window.

5

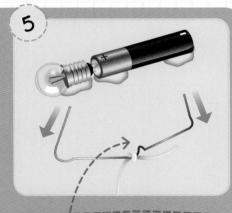

Tie one end carefully around the paper clip and the other end around the handle that opens away from the battery. The alarm is set: if someone opens the window, the light will go off.

HOW DOES IT WORK?

At its heart, this alarm relies on an electrical circuit, a flow of electrons. The circuit lights the bulb as it passes through it, and the bulb goes out if the circuit is broken. Keeping the string tight (between the battery and the window) means that the slightest pull on the window will yank the string.

And when the string is pulled, it pulls the paper clip "circuit creator" from the battery. With the circuit broken, the light goes off.

And that's evidence that someone (or something) had been fiddling with the window. There's your evidence. Now for some more detective work!

REAL LIFE SCIENCE

Most intruder alarms involve some sort of electrical circuit, which an intruder upsets in some way. The alarm in this experiment begins with the circuit in place (and the light on). The evidence that someone had been nosing around comes from seeing the light off. Other alarms work in the opposite way: a disturbance to a door or window creates a circuit, which triggers a light or a sound.

WHAT HAPPENS IF...?

Think about it. What would happen if you made exactly the same sort of alarm and tied it to a window or door that opened in instead of out? Why not make a prediction and test it?

The Floating Clip

Looking for one of the quickest experiments in the book? Here's one that still manages to demonstrate two important scientific principles, almost as fast as you can say "water molecules" and "surface tension."

YOU WILL NEED

- Small paper clips
- Water
- Sink or basin
- Dishwashing liquid

1 Fill the sink or basin until it's nearly full.

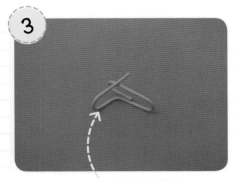

2 Wait until the water is really still and then let go of a paper clip about 1 inch (3 cm) above the water: it sinks.

3 Bend another clip so that the longer loop forms a right angle with the rest of the clip.

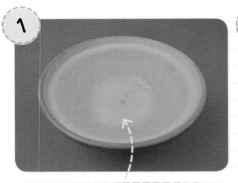

4 Hold the bent clip downward, with the long loop forming a "shelf." Balance another paper clip on top.

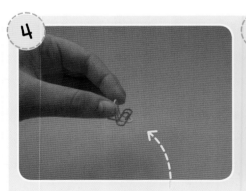

5 With the paper clip resting on it, lower the "shelf" clip into the water carefully and slide it down and out of the water once the other clip stays and floats.

6 Observe this paper clip floating calmly... until you add a couple of drops of dishwashing liquid. Then it immediately sinks.

When hydrogen and oxygen combine to form water, the result is called a molecule. That means any combination of atoms that stick together. Two hydrogen atoms combine with every one oxygen atom to form a water molecule. And it's trillions of these molecules that join together to form what we see as water.

An electrical force called surface tension holds water molecules together tightly along the water surface. Some light objects (like the paper clip) can even rest on the water because of the surface tension. But the chemicals in the soapy liquid "short circuit" that bond, so the paper clip is no longer held up.

REAL LIFE SCIENCE

Getting water to stick together, or to be pushed away, is really important for many industries and products. Some of the same chemistry that broke up the surface tension in this experiment plays a part in designing waterproof clothing, for example. After all, the designers were looking for something that would push water away!

WHAT HAPPENS IF...?

Try varying the experiment. With the water still soapy, try lowering another paper clip carefully onto the surface. Will it stay floating? Why is that?

Make an iceberg

YOU WILL NEED

- A balloon
- Water
- Freezer
- Sink or basin
- Ruler
- Plastic tray

You may have heard people say, "It's just the tip of the iceberg." This means that there's a lot more to something than meets the eye. Just how much of an iceberg can you see, anyway? You can find out in your kitchen, although you will need to start the experiment the night before.

1

Fill the balloon with water from a faucet and tie it shut.

2

Put the balloon in the freezer, making sure there's enough room for it to keep its shape.

3

Leave overnight and remove the balloon: it will be full of solid ice.

4
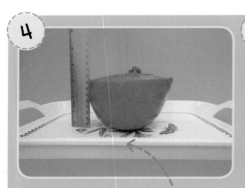
Set the balloon on a plastic tray and measure its height. You might be able to peel the balloon from the ice, but it doesn't matter if you can't.

5

Fill the sink or basin about two-thirds with water and set the "iceberg" in it. It should now be floating.

6

Carefully measure the height from the water level to the top of the iceberg. Now compare it with the overall height that you measured earlier.

HOW DOES IT WORK?

Real icebergs form when bits of glacier (frozen rivers) break off into the sea. They form floating chunks that tower up to 165 feet (50 m) above the surface of the water. But as with your home-made iceberg, about 90 percent of these giants lie underwater.

The reason boils down to density, which is how much something weighs in a given volume (or space). When water freezes, it expands and becomes less dense than its liquid state. About 10 percent less dense, in fact. And that 10 percent difference pops up (literally) in the bit that floats above the water.

WHAT HAPPENS IF...?

Wait! Our experiment has the iceberg floating in fresh water, but real icebergs are floating in the sea. Surely that's a big difference? Well, not really: salt water is a little bit denser, so the iceberg would poke out a tiny bit more... but not that much. Add some salt to your water and record any differences.

REAL LIFE SCIENCE

The most famous sinking ship in history is the Titanic, which went down in April 1912, with the loss of more than 1,500 people. The ship struck an iceberg in the cold waters off Canada. Modern ships have electronic equipment to detect icebergs in the dark, including the hidden mass underwater. They are far safer around icebergs than the supposedly "unsinkable" Titanic.

A Lot of Hot Air?

YOU WILL NEED

- Empty plastic drink bottle (about 12 fl oz/ 330 ml)
- Balloon
- Freezer
- Water from the hot faucet
- Sink or basin

Do you ever get tired or out of breath from blowing up balloons? Wouldn't it be great to find a way to get them to inflate themselves? Well, you can use science to do some of the job. It might not be quick, but it's a good way to save your breath for a while!

1

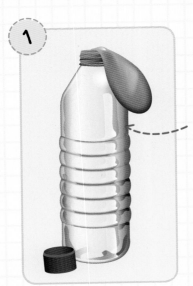

Feed the balloon over the top of the empty bottle. Make sure it covers all the twists in the mouth of the bottle and is firmly in place.

Put the bottle (with the attached balloon) into the freezer for 30 minutes.

2

3

Just before the 30 minutes is up, fill the sink or basin about two-thirds up with water from the hot faucet.

4

Take the bottle from the freezer and stand it in the hot water, making sure the water does not get into the bottle.

5

Watch the balloon begin to inflate by itself!

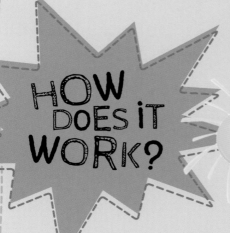

HOW DOES IT WORK?

Air is a gas made up of many, many molecules (which themselves are combinations of atoms.) Those molecules move around more, and take up more space, when they are warm. They move around less, and take up less space, as they cool.

The air inside the bottle and balloon "shrank" when it was in the freezer, but expanded again when it came out... and expanded enough to start filling the balloon when it got warmed in the hot water.

TOP TIPS!

Water from the hot faucet can be VERY hot sometimes. Be careful!

WHAT HAPPENS IF...?

Not convinced? Take several balloons and repeat the experiment a number of times but at different temperatures: say, outside on a cold day or in the refrigerator. Record your results. You can also try attaching a balloon to a bottle and simply leaving it where it is, on the table at room temperature, for 30 minutes. What do you think will happen?

REAL LIFE SCIENCE

Many liquids take up more space when they have been warmed up to produce a gas. A steam engine works by heating water until it becomes a gas (water vapor.) The water vapor expands, pushing bits of machinery back and forth or around and around... and it can even power something as big and heavy as a train!

The ice-cube Hoist

YOU WILL NEED

- Ice cube
- Saucer or small plate
- String
- Scissors
- Salt
- Teaspoon

Want an experiment that can also double as a magic trick at a birthday party? How about asking people whether they think you can lift an ice cube without touching it, using only a piece of string.

1 Set the ice cube on the saucer or plate.

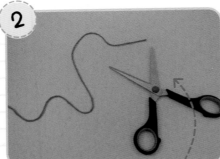

2 Cut a length of string about as long as your arm (from the elbow down).

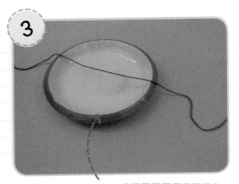

3 Lay the string across the ice cube, with an equal length either side of it.

4 Hold both ends of the string and lift. The ice cube will stay in place.

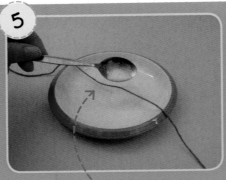

5 Lay the string across the ice cube again. Sprinkle about half a teaspoon of salt over the ice cube and wait for 30 seconds.

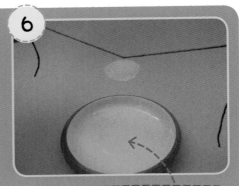

6 Hold the string at both ends again and carefully lift. The ice cube rises up!

Maybe you've seen people spreading salt over their paths in freezing weather, or seen trucks sprinkling it on roads to make them less icy. That's because the chemicals in salt react with water to lower its freezing point. It remains a liquid even a bit below 32°F (0°C), the normal freezing point.

You did something similar. The salt lowered the melting point of the ice cube, allowing the string to sink in. But then the salty water became more dilute and some of it ran off the ice cube. The water on top became solid ice once more, locking the string inside.

REAL LIFE SCIENCE

Salt works well to keep roads clear, but it needs to be used carefully. Too much salt can mix with melted ice and damage the plants and animals that live nearby.

WHAT HAPPENS IF...?

Can you find a recipe to make ice cream? Cream needs to be frozen quickly to make good ice cream. That's why, when you make ice cream at home, you often use salt. The container with the cream and sugar is placed inside anther container of salt and water. The frozen salt-water is colder than normal ice, helping the cream mixture to freeze faster.

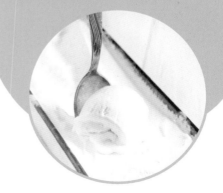

Egg in a Bottle

You've probably heard about, or even seen, a model ship inside a bottle. It takes special tools and LOTS of patience. But you can do better than that: get a hard-boiled egg inside a narrow-necked bottle in an instant!

YOU WILL NEED

- A hard-boiled egg
- Cooking oil
- A glass bottle with a mouth just narrower than the width of the egg
- Matches
- Strip of newspaper torn to roughly 1 inch x 4 inches (3 cm x 10 cm)
- Kitchen towel

1

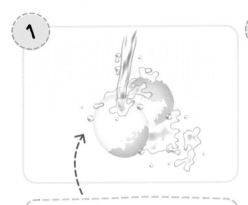

Peel the egg. If you do it under running cold water it makes it easier. Rest the egg, smaller side down, on the mouth of the bottle to check the fit.

2

Put the egg to one side, Dip the kitchen towel in some oil and rub the inside of the bottle's mouth. This will help the egg slip through.

3

Have an adult light one end of the newspaper strip and drop it into the bottle (with the flaming bit pointing down.)

4

As soon as the paper's inside, put the egg back in place on top.

5

Within seconds, you'll see the egg wiggle a little and then get sucked inside the bottle.

HOW DOES IT WORK?

This experiment may be simple, but it still demonstrates several scientific ideas at once. We're talking about heat, density and pressure. And it's air that's doing all the work. The burning paper warmed the air inside the bottle. As it warmed, the air became less dense and expanded. Some even rose from the bottle.

Plugging the bottle with the egg trapped the air inside. The air began to cool and take up less space inside the bottle. It wasn't pressing out so much. But the outside air was still "full strength" and it pushed the egg down as it went to fill the space inside.

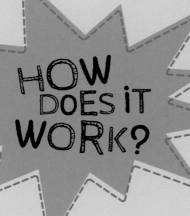

TOP TiPS!

An adult must handle the matches and burning strip of paper.

WHAT HAPPENS IF...?

Try doing this experiment in reverse. Put a small ice cube inside a bottle to cool the air inside. When it's melted, plug the mouth of the bottle with a ping-pong ball and wrap your hands around the bottle (to warm the air inside.) Predict what will happen... and why.

REAL LiFE SCiENCE

Vacuum cleaners work by using the difference in air pressure. The fan inside the cleaner moves air forward quickly, which lowers the air pressure inside the vacuum cleaner. (You lower the air pressure in a straw when you suck.) The "normal pressure" air outside pushes in toward the cleaner, carrying dust and dirt with it.

Water Mix-Up

Changing something's temperature can change the way it looks and feels. Just think of melting wax from candles or liquid water turning into ice cubes. But what happens when one version of a substance bumps into a warmer (or colder) version of itself? The result might be colorful...

1

Fill one jar with cold water and the other with hot water.

2

Pour several drops of blue coloring into the cold water and stir. Do the same with red coloring in the hot water.

3

Put the jar with hot water in the bowl.

4

Place the cardboard over the top of the jar with cold water. Check to make sure it hangs beyond all of the rim.

5

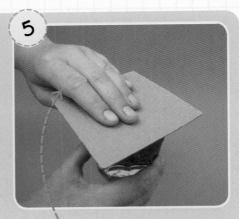

Holding the cold jar with one hand, press your other hand down on the cardboard so that it is firmly in place.

6

Carry the cold jar over to the bowl and rest it over the hot-water jar. Remove your hand from the cardboard (it will stick to the rim) and lower the cold jar down.

7

Match the two jars up so that the rims are in line, and then hold the top jar while you carefully slide the cardboard out. Don't worry if a little water spills out.

8

You should see the two colors merging, with blue sinking down to meet red rising up. After a few minutes both bottles should have a purple color.

9

Carefully dismantle this arrangement, letting the water spill into the bowl.

10

Fill the jars up again, once more adding red coloring to the hot water and blue to the cold.

11

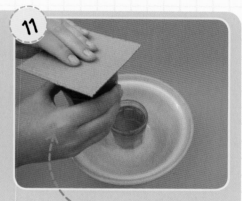

This time, place the blue (cold-water) jar in the bowl and place the cardboard over the red (hot-water) jar.

12

Balance the jars as you did earlier, then carefully slide the cardboard out... and wait. The colors remain separate.

Continued

HOW DOES IT WORK?

This experiment is a colorful demonstration of density, which is something's weight within a given volume, or space. Water becomes less dense when it becomes warmer. The water in this experiment sits in a given volume, the identical volume of the jars.

So when you placed the blue (cold) water above the red (hot) water, the heavier cold water sank down and merged with the hot water, pushing some of it up. The waters merged, and so did their colors. But when the less dense (lighter) hot water was already on top in the second stage, the waters and their colors remained separate.

TOP TIPS!

The hot water should be hot, but not too hot! Be careful not to burn yourself.

WHAT HAPPENS IF...?

You know that this experiment focuses on density and temperature. Try doing it a little differently, with slightly less difference in temperature between the water jars. Take the temperature of each jar each time you perform the experiment. Can you predict when the difference in temperature will become too small to stop the colors blending?

REAL LIFE SCIENCE

Scientists who study the sea often measure the temperature of ocean currents. Even small changes affect the density and movement of the water. Differences in some of the currents in the Pacific Ocean can affect the weather in the entire planet.

Baked Alaska

"Mmm. For dessert you'll be having some baked ice cream." Baked ice cream?! Impossible! Well, not really, if you're able to get science to team up with cooking skills. Ask an adult to help with this experiment.

YOU WILL NEED

- 1 quart (945 ml) vanilla ice cream (sold as a block, not in a tub)
- One 8 inch (20 cm) sponge cake
- 3 egg whites
- 7 ounces (200 g) of super-fine sugar
- Cream of tartar
- Teaspoon
- Tablespoon
- Food mixer
- Freezer
- Oven
- Large mixing bowl
- Baking pan
- Tin foil
- Spatula

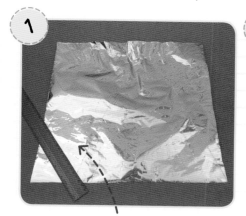

1

Tear a 16-inch (40-cm) length of foil and lay it on a counter or table.

2

Lay the cake flat in the middle of the foil.

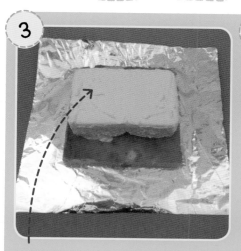

3

Place the block of ice cream in the middle of the cake.

4

The cake should jut out about 1 inch (3 cm) beyond the ice cream. Trim the cake or the ice cream to fit.

5

Loosely cover with another length of foil and leave in the freezer for 15 minutes (to freeze solid.)

6

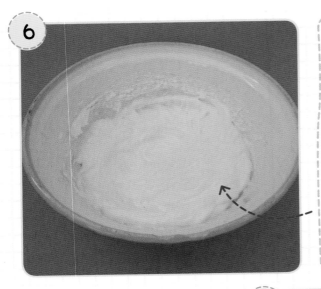

Preheat oven to 425°F (220°C.) When the 15 minutes is nearly up, beat the egg whites and cream of tartar in the mixer until the mixture forms peaks that are becoming stiff.

7

Add the sugar, one tablespoon at a time, to the mixture. Beat after each tablespoon.

8

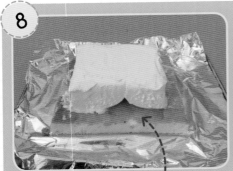

Transfer the cake and ice cream to a baking pan, removing the loose foil on top but leaving the foil base.

9

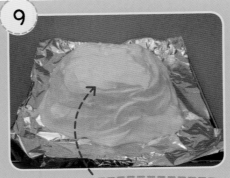

Use the spatula to spread the egg-white mixture over all of the ice cream and cake. Make sure that everything is covered, even some of the baking pan next to it.

10

Make some decorative swirls in the mixture and place in the center of the oven for five minutes.

11

Serve in slices. The outside will be cooked brown, but the ice cream will still be frozen!

HOW DOES IT WORK?

This experiment is all about insulation, but the other way round from the way we'd expect. Normally we think of insulation as a way of keeping heat in, as with a coat, in a house or other building.

Baked Alaska is about keeping heat out, so it won't melt the ice cream. And it's the outside egg-white layer, called a meringue, that does the insulating. Beating it added lots and lots of air, making it fluff right up. And air is a good insulator. Just think of how snug you feel in a cosy duvet, which is mainly full of air!

TOP TIPS!

Ask an adult to help you beat the egg whites and to use the oven. Your adult can also help you to eat your Baked Alaska!

WHAT HAPPENS IF...?

What if you cooked it longer, but on a lower temperature? The ice cream would melt. The only thing you wanted to cook was the outside layer. Any longer, even at a lower temperature, would mean that the warm air would have time to penetrate inside. Just as it does on a warm day if you leave a popsicle to melt on a plate.

REAL LIFE SCIENCE

The Inuit people who live near the North Pole are famous for their igloos, small houses and shelters built from blocks of snow. Igloos work like the meringue on the outside of the Baked Alaska. The snow is full of air pockets, which work as insulators. With igloos, though, the idea of the insulation is to keep the heat in, not out.

Hot-air Balloon

YOU WILL NEED

- 2 sheets each of red and blue tissue paper: 20 inches x 30 inches (50 cm x 75 cm)
- Water-based glue
- Scissors
- Marker pen
- Thin cardboard
- Blow-dryer

Take a step back more than 200 years and up a meter or two with your own version of some ground-breaking technology. It ultimately led to jet planes and helicopters. But this balloon can take off from your own house!

1

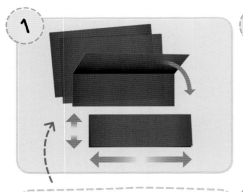

Fold each sheet in half along the short side, so that each measures 10 inches x 30 inches (25 cm x 75 cm). Lay each down with the folded edge toward you.

2

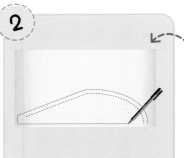

Copy the template design (shown here) onto the piece of thin cardboard, making the upright side on the left 2 inches (5 cm) tall and the other straight edge 24 inches (60 cm) long.

3

Cut out the template and then trace its outside shape along each of the four pieces of tissue paper. The 24-inch (60-cm) straight edge should run along the fold of the tissue paper.

4

Carefully cut each of the pieces of tissue paper and unfold. Glue the four pieces together, overlapping the pieces as shown here. Make sure that the mouth of the balloon, where the 2-inch (5-cm) sections join, can still open.

5

Place the balloon so that its mouth is just above an upward-pointing blow-dryer. Turn it on using the "warm" setting, Watch the balloon fill up and then release it.

HOW DOES IT WORK?

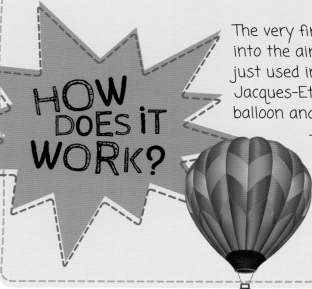

The very first type of man-made object to carry passengers into the air used some of the same methods that you've just used in this experiment. In 1783, Joseph-Ralf and Jacques-Etienne Montgolfier took off in the first hot-air balloon and floated over astounded observers in France.

They used a simple principle. By warming the air inside the balloon, they made it less dense than the surrounding air. That meant that it would "float" on the outside air as long as the air inside was warm. You've done exactly the same thing with your balloon and blow-dryer.

WHAT HAPPENS IF...?

You can see the difference that heat makes if you fill the balloon with air when the blow-dryer is set to cool. Any idea about what might happen? (Or not happen?)

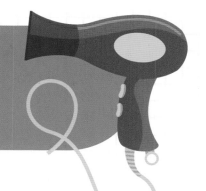

REAL LIFE SCIENCE

Hot-air balloons remain popular ways of enjoying sights from above... but you'd need huge balloons and lots of furnaces to float more than a few people along. That's why modern airships use gases such as helium inside their "balloon" bits. Like heated air, they are less dense than the air around them—"lighter than air," in fact.

TOP TIPS!

- Ask an adult to hold the balloon above the blow-dryer as you fill the balloon.
- Take care not to let the balloon get too close to the blow-dryer.

The Melting Ice Caps

If you're interested in the environment, you will know that the ice caps by the North and South poles are getting smaller. But did you know that the ice caps' color helps to keep the poles cool? The smaller they become, the warmer it will get. How does that work, exactly? The answer might be on your windowsill.

1

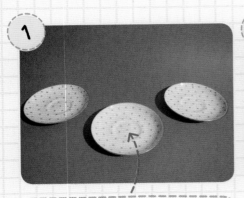

Line up the saucers on the sunny windowsill.

2

Put a piece of fabric in each. It doesn't matter in which order.

3

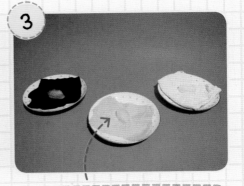

Place an ice cube in the middle of each piece of fabric.

4

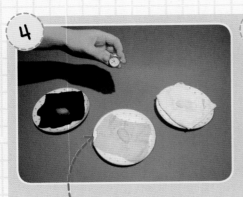

Make sure that the ice cubes are all in full sunlight and wait five minutes.

5

Check on the ice cubes and observe which one has melted most.

6

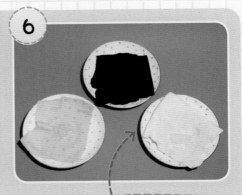

Remain by the ice cubes to see how long it takes for each to melt. The one on the black fabric should disappear first... and the one on the white last.

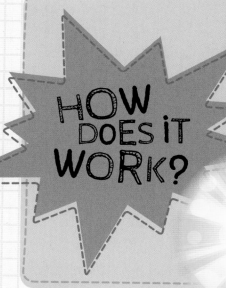

HOW DOES IT WORK?

It all boils down to energy. Heat and light are both forms of energy, which is sent out by a process called radiation. Some of this radiation we can see (visible light.) Others are invisible to our eyes but we can see their effect (ultraviolet light causes sunburn.)

What we see as colors give us a clue about how an object absorbs this light radiation. Black absorbs all types of light radiation and turns some of that into heat. White reflects light, so it turns very little into heat. And colors in between absorb more than white but less than black.

WHAT HAPPENS IF...?

Do exactly the same experiment but at night, with the lights turned off (except when you enter the room to check on the melting.) What differences do you notice between the colors? Or are there any differences?

REAL LIFE SCIENCE

This effect can be seen in the speed a glacier melts. The ice forming the glacier is white, reflecting the sunlight. But once part of the glacier melts, exposing rock, the glacier starts to melt more quickly. The dark rock means more sunlight is converted into heat. And some of the heat passes along the rock and melts the ice near it... which exposes even more dark rock. And so it continues.

Magic Fire Extinguisher

YOU WILL NEED

- Small mixing bowl, about 1 quart (950 ml)
- 2 tablespoons of vinegar
- 3 tablespoons of baking soda
- 2 tea light candles
- Matches
- Small measuring cup, with spout

Balloons and airships float above us because they're "lighter than air". Here's an experiment that shows you how to create a gas that's "heavier than air". Get it right and you might turn out to be a firefighter later in life.

1

Add baking soda to the mixing bowl; swirl the bowl around to spread it out evenly.

2

Add the vinegar to the measuring cup.

3

Place the two candles in the bowl, as close to the center as possible.

4

Get an adult to light both candles.

5

Wait about 15 seconds to make sure both candles are burning strongly, then pour the vinegar evenly into the bowl, but not directly on to the candles.

6

Watch what happens, especially with the flames—they should go out quickly!

HOW DOES IT WORK?

This experiment is a great way to "see" how gases behave, even if they're invisible. Air is made up of many different gases, but it's the oxygen in it that fires need to burn. When you added the vinegar to the baking soda in the bowl, the reaction produced another invisible gas—carbon dioxide.

That's where things get even more interesting. Carbon dioxide is denser (heavier) than air, so it sinks down below the air. As the bowl started to fill up with carbon dioxide, the air was pushed out. And without the oxygen inside the air, the flames in the candles were extinguished.

TOP TIPS!

Only an adult should use the matches in this experiment.

WHAT HAPPENS IF...?

Try doing the same experiment but using candles that are a little bit taller. You could use birthday candles resting in poster putty. Do you think it will take longer for the candles to go out?

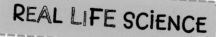

REAL LIFE SCIENCE

Putting out fires is an important and dangerous job. And depending on what's burning, firefighters have to find the right way to extinguish the flames. Carbon dioxide, held under high pressure, is one type of fire extinguisher and it's often used on fires involving electrical equipment.

The Carbon Dragon

With just a bit of scientific trickery, you can turn an ordinary household rubber glove into a scary-looking dragon. This is another experiment that looks like magic, but it depends on chemistry. You might have to choose between a magician's cape and a scientist's white coat!

1 Draw a scary dragon's face on the glove, using the fingers to show the dragon's horns and plumes of smoke.

2 Add 3 tablespoons of vinegar to the glass.

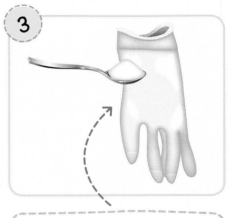

3 Hold the glove so that the fingers point down and sprinkle 2 tablespoons of baking soda into it. Make sure that it gets right into the fingers.

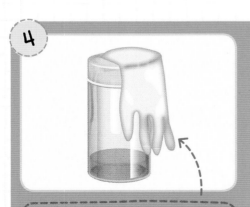

4 Keeping the glove floppy, with fingers pointing down, fit the wrist of the glove over the rim of the glass.

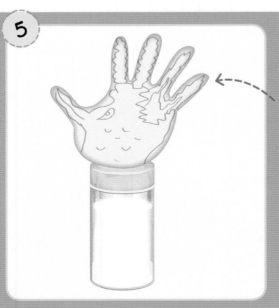

5 Lift the tips of the glove fingers upright so that the baking soda falls into the glass. Watch as the glove begins to inflate, getting larger and more upright. The dragon will get a new, terrifying look!

HOW DOES IT WORK?

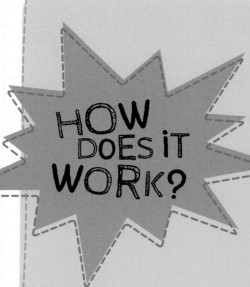

You're examining more than one scientific effect with this experiment! You already know that combining different materials can produce a third. In this experiment you have combined a liquid (the vinegar) with a solid (the baking soda) and produced a gas (carbon dioxide). It's the carbon dioxide that builds up thanks to the reaction, filling the flexible rubber glove and giving the face its scary character.

This experiment also shows the importance of choosing the right material. Rubber can stretch, so the glove can blow up like a balloon and let your dragon come to life!

How would the experiment work if you used a glove made of wool instead of rubber? Make a prediction and record your findings.

WHAT HAPPENS IF...?

REAL LIFE SCIENCE

Materials that behave in similar ways are often grouped together. Baking soda is part of a group known as bases, and they often react strongly with another group, known as acids. Vinegar contains acid, but so do many foods, especially citrus fruits such as oranges, lemons, and limes. This experiment would also work well with lemon juice instead of vinegar.

Taking the Plunge

- 2 identical sink plungers ("plumber's friends")
- Water
- Kitchen towel

And the winner of the "Quickest Experiment in the Book Award" goes to... (drum roll) ... "Taking the Plunge"! It's true that this is a simple experiment to do, but it's mighty hard to undo. You'll soon see why.

1

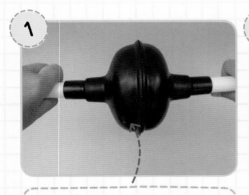

Hold the plungers so that the rubber domes just meet each other.

2

Pull the plungers apart. You should be able to do this easily.

3

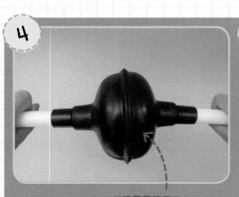

Wet a kitchen towel and rub it along the rubber rims of both plungers.

4

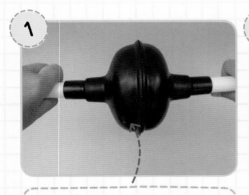

Line the plungers up again so that they almost, but not quite, meet. Push in on both of them. You might even hear air rushing out from between them.

5

Continue pressing in and slide the domes together so that they line up exactly.

6

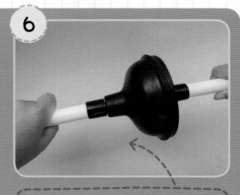

The two plungers should feel stuck together. Try pulling them apart—it's almost impossible!

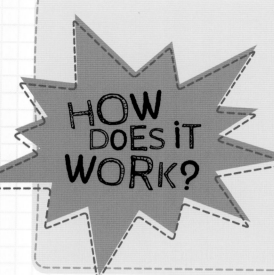

HOW DOES IT WORK?

This experiment demonstrates what happens when air is removed. Scientists call such a condition a vacuum. You forced the air out from inside both rubber domes. And you had to be accurate and have good timing to leave a little crack between them (to let air out) before sliding them back (to stop air from coming in). So, for a while, there was no air inside to push out, but the normal pressure of air was pushing in. That's what locked the plungers together. When you tried to pull them apart, you were fighting against the air pressure.

TOP TIPS!

To separate the plungers, try to slide them apart instead of pulling them.

WHAT HAPPENS IF...?

What if you hadn't pumped all of the air out to create a vacuum? Well, that's exactly what you did in Steps 1 and 2. It was easy to pull the plungers apart because the air inside the domes was pressing out with the same force as the outside air pressing in.

REAL LIFE SCIENCE

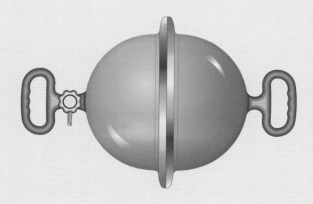

This experiment was first performed by Otto Von Guericke in Magdeburg, Germany, in 1654. He pushed two copper domes together, pumped the air out and sealed the domes with grease to prevent air from getting in. The domes couldn't be pulled apart, even with a team of thirty horses. They're remembered as the Magdeburg Hemispheres (a hemisphere is a dome shape).

Vinegar Rocket

5, 4, 3, 2, 1... BLAST OFF! Gases, even invisible ones, can pack a real punch, as you'll soon see. Make sure you ask an adult to help you with this dramatic experiment, and check out the "Top Tips" before you get started.

YOU WILL NEED

- Goggles
- Tablespoon
- Teaspoon
- Candies cylinder with snap top lid
- Baking soda
- Vinegar
- Scissors
- Clear tape
- Piece of cardboard
- Ruler

1

Cut 3 right-angled triangles from the cardboard, with equal sides about 1 inch (3 cm) long.

2

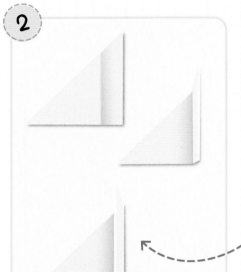

Fold one of those equal sides back about ⅜ inch (1 cm) on each triangle.

3

Turn the canister or cylinder upside-down (resting on the lid) and tape the cardboard triangles on to make three fins.

4

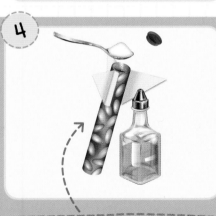

Turn the canister right-side up and remove the lid. Add 1 tablespoon of vinegar. Ask an adult to add ½ teaspoon of baking soda to the canister.

5

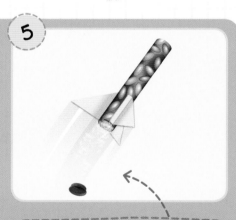

Click the lid back on and then turn the canister upside-down. It should now be standing in the same position it had in Step 3. Stand well back and wait 10 to 15 seconds for the rocket to take off!

HOW DOES IT WORK?

Your rocket blasted off because of the power of a gas (carbon dioxide) that you helped produce when the baking soda reacted with the acid contained in the vinegar. In fact, it's the speed of that reaction—how fast the carbon dioxide was produced—that packs the power.

The amount of gas produced is far, far greater than the volume of the cylinder. So the gas pressed against the sides of the canister harder and harder (as more of it was produced)... and then found the "weak spot" which was the snap-on lid. That's why the lid got blown off like a rocket!

WHAT HAPPENS IF...?

What do you suppose would happen if you used water instead of vinegar and a fizzing vitamin tablet instead of baking soda? There's one way of finding out!

TOP TIPS!

- An adult (wearing goggles) should load the rocket and launch it.

- This project is messy! Do it outdoors.

- Wait at least a minute if the rocket doesn't launch before an adult checks on it.

REAL LIFE SCIENCE

You experience a version of this experiment thousands of times whenever you ride in a car. Small amounts of fuel are ignited by a car's spark plugs. The fuel turns into a gas, which pushes pistons... which in turn propel the car forward. And it all happens even faster in a racing car!

Pencil-proof Bag

Science is about curiosity and finding answers to difficult questions, even if the answers set up even more questions. Do you suppose any scientist has asked "What will happen if I stick a pencil into that plastic bag full of water?" Maybe it's time you asked that question—and discovered the surprising answer.

YOU WILL NEED

- Clear plastic sandwich bag (zip-lock types work well)
- 3 sharp pencils
- Water
- Large mixing bowl or sink

1

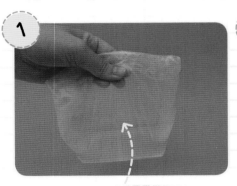

Fill a sandwich bag just over halfway with water. Pinch it shut (or zip-lock it) so that you can hold it between your index finger and thumb.

2

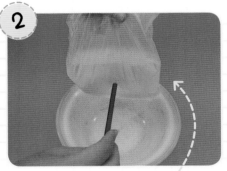

Hold the bag carefully over the bowl or sink and slowly pierce it below the water line with the pencil.

3

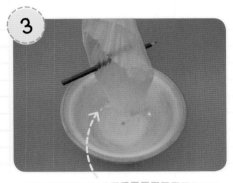

Continue slowly pressing that pencil so that it passes through the bag completely; stop when you have some of it sticking out of both sides.

4

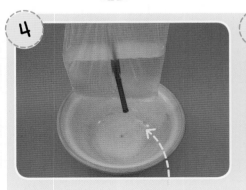

Take your hand away from the pencil, which should remain stuck in the bag with no water leaking.

5

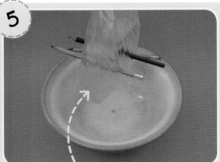

Keeping the first pencil in place, slide the other two pencils through the bag until they jut out from both sides.

6

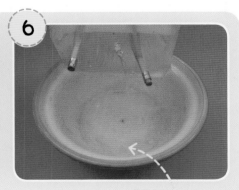

While still holding the bag from above, remove the first pencil and watch water come streaming out.

HOW DOES IT WORK?

You're learning something about a very popular material in this experiment: plastic. Most types of plastic are made of chains of molecules called polymers. Those polymer chains are flexible, so they stretch out and tighten back up easily.

The sharp end of the pencil pushed some of these chains apart as it poked into the bag. The plastic polymers kept stretching as the point got wider, then tightened up around the pencil. And it was tight enough to plug any leaks. It's a bit like when you pull a sweater down over your head. The neck-hole gets wider to let your head through and then tightens again once it's on.

TOP TIPS!

This experiment is only messy at the end, but take care not to do it near anything that could be damaged by water.

WHAT HAPPENS IF...?

Blow up a balloon and tie it. Ask an adult to push an oiled cooking skewer into the bit of the balloon next to the knot and then out the far end (where the rubber is still dark and thick). The balloon won't pop! It's made of polymers that moved and made way for the skewer.

REAL LIFE SCIENCE

The flexibility of polymers makes them useful in many industries, ranging from cars and trucks to artificial fibers in clothing. For example, lycra or elastene is a synthetic fiber known for its amazing elasticity. It is used a great deal in sportswear and is particularly popular with professional cyclists.

Plastic Milk?

You know that milk can turn into yogurt or cheese. But can it really turn into plastic? Well... with just a little bit of help from you, it can turn into something that could pass for plastic. Ask an adult to help you with this experiment.

YOU WILL NEED

- Whole milk (not reduced or low fat)
- Measuring cup
- Teaspoon
- White vinegar
- Saucepan
- Sieve about 6 inches (15 cm) in diameter
- Mixing bowl about 6 inches (15 cm) in diameter
- Dinner plate or dish

1

Pour one cup (225 ml) of milk into a saucepan and ask an adult to heat it gently.

2

When the milk is hot, but not boiling, take the pan off the heat. Stir in 4 teaspoons of vinegar.

3

Continue stirring for a minute.

4

Rest the sieve on the mixing bowl and pour the milk through it. White lumps should remain in the strainer after the liquid has gone through.

5

Turn the lumps onto a plate or dish and let them cool for a few minutes. Press the lumps into a rubbery ball or into any shape you choose. Set it aside and in a day or two it will harden into a tough plastic form.

HOW DOES IT WORK?

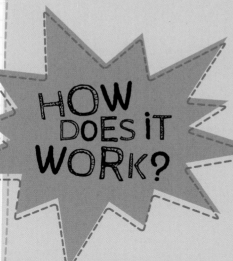

You've probably heated milk for cocoa or oatmeal lots of times and it's never turned into rubber or plastic, even when it has cooled. So the difference seems to be adding vinegar. And that's where the chemistry kicks in, helping to change one familiar material (milk) into something that looks and feels like another (rubber or plastic).

The vinegar contains an acid, which causes the milk to separate into a liquid (which poured through the sieve) and a solid made of fats and a protein called casein. And this casein is made up of molecules that link up (and behave) like plastic molecules.

WHAT HAPPENS IF...?

It was the acid in the vinegar that kick-started this experiment. Why not try the experiment again with lemon juice (which also contains an acid), to see whether it would still work. As scientists always advise: "Make a prediction and test your results."

TOP TIPS!

You need an adult present at all times in this experiment, especially the heating on the stove.

REAL LIFE SCIENCE

Casein, the key to the plastic side of this experiment, is used in lots of ways from making paints and glues to helping dentists make teeth stronger. Have you ever taken a bite of pizza and a string of cheese just gets longer and longer? That's down to the casein in the pizza's cheese topping.

Stacking Liquids

You can picture all sorts of things being stacked up in your kitchens—plates, saucers, recipe books, even pancakes. But how about stacking some liquids? Not bottles of liquids—the liquids themselves. Impossible? Not with some science to help.

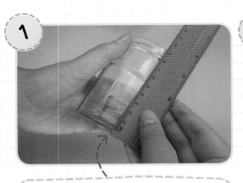

1 Measure the height of the jar and then divide that number by three. Measure that one-third distance up from the bottom of the jar and make a mark with the marker pen.

2 Measure the same amount up from that mark and make another mark. The jar is now marked in equal thirds.

3 Carefully pour honey up to the first mark.

4 Next pour oil until it reaches the second mark. It works better if you let the oil run down the inside of the jar.

5 Finish by adding water until it nearly reaches the top. You should now have a stack of liquids.

6 Drop in the coin, then the grape, and finally the cornflake—they should settle in the bottom, middle, and top layers.

HOW DOES iT WORK?

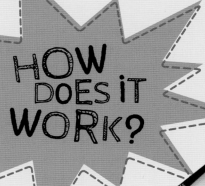

In this experiment, the liquids stack up according to their density. The densest (heaviest in a given volume) sink to the bottom and the others stack up above it, in descending order of density. You can see that the honey has the greatest density, then the water, and finally the oil (which stays on the top).

The objects you dropped will pass through any liquid that is less dense, but settle when they reach something that's denser than them. It's tied in with the reason why some objects float on the sea and others just sink.

WHAT HAPPENS IF...?

If you still have the lid from the jar, tighten it and then slowly turn the jar upside-down. Make a prediction about what you think will happen. Wait a few minutes and see how your predictions worked out.

REAL LIFE SCIENCE

The oil that sometimes spills from oil wells and tankers has a lower density than seawater. That means that it floats on the surface. If clean-up crews can reach the spill before it washes up on shore, they try to gather it from the surface of the ocean. It's difficult and expensive, but a lot better than having the oil harm wildlife and ruin beaches.

The Ice Slice

We could all learn about life by following the example of ice cubes. Ice cubes?! Just watch how a simple ice cube deals with pressure when things are down to the wire. This experiment works best in a cool room.

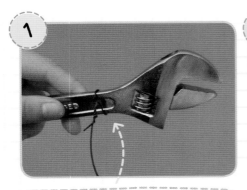

1 Loop and twist each end of the wire to a wrench or other object and see how the arrangement hangs if you have your hand under the middle of the wire.

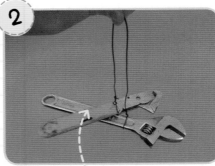

2 Adjust and retighten wire until each wrench hangs evenly. Set the cork securely in the mouth of the bottle.

3 Ask an adult to use a knife to trim the bottom of the cork if it's too big for the mouth.

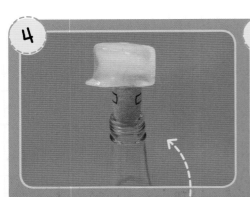

4 Lay the ice cube on the cork, making sure that it's securely in place.

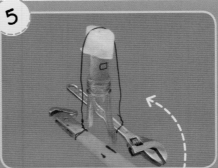

5 Lay the wire across the top of the ice cube so that the wrenches (or other objects) hang down on either side of the bottle.

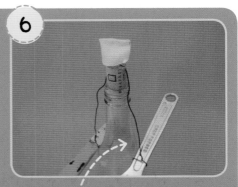

6 Wait and observe how the wire is pulled right through the ice cube. But in the end the ice cube doesn't seem to have changed.

HOW DOES IT WORK?

Aha! Here's one where there are some real arguments, and maybe your contribution will help scientists finally decide on the answer. First, the bit that everyone agrees on. The water freezes again after the wire has passed through. But why? And why does it melt in the first place?

One theory is that the pressure lowers the melting point of water and when the pressure is released (the wire has passed), the water freezes again. The other says that the wire conducts (passes on) heat, just enough to melt the ice briefly. What do you think?

WHAT HAPPENS IF...?

You can do your bit to solve the "ice cube mystery" by mixing things up a little. Try doing the experiment in your refrigerator (opening the door from time to time to observe). And what would happen if you did the experiment in your freezer? Does that tell you anything about the wire conducting heat?

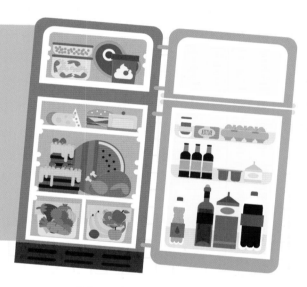

REAL LIFE SCIENCE

A similar argument rages about what happens when people are ice-skating. Is it friction (the skate rubbing against the ice) that melts just a bit of ice, so that they slide? Or is it the pressure of the skate against the ice lowering its melting point?

Stepping on Eggshells

When you hear people say "it's like walking on eggshells" you know what they mean – you need to be careful because they break so easily. But if you use a little science, you can get those shells to support a lot of weight. Impossible? Maybe not...

YOU WILL NEED

- 4 eggs, plus a couple extra in case of breakages
- Clear tape
- Small, sharp scissors
- Several large, heavy books, such as telephone books
- Small mixing bowl
- Spoon

1

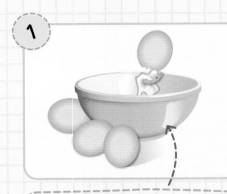

Remove the tiniest shell fragments to empty the eggs into the bowl. You can use the contents of the bowl later for cooking.

Keeping a bowl underneath, hold the wider end of each egg in turn and tap at the narrower end with the spoon until you open a crack.

Carefully wind some tape around the widest part of each egg.

2

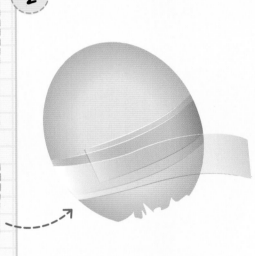

3

Use the scissors to cut around the middle of the tape to create four "egg domes" of equal size.

4

Lay the four egg domes on a counter or table, forming a rectangle.

5

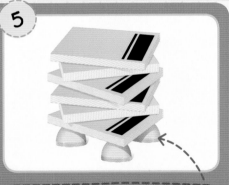

Slowly lay a book on the "egg rectangle." The shells won't break! See how many more books you can add until they finally give way.

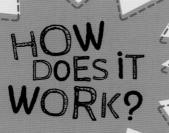

HOW DOES IT WORK?

If you were to look under a hen sitting on an egg, you'd see that it was pointing up. Otherwise the hen could easily break it. That's because eggs have one of the strongest designs possible - they're dome-shaped.

A dome is able to spread the pressure from above (say, the weight of those books, or a hen) evenly through the entire structure. There's no single part of the dome that has to do more work than any other. That's why domes and arches (which also spread pressure) are so important for architects designing large buildings.

WHAT HAPPENS IF...?

What if the eggshells are pointing sideways, not vertically? To do this you need to pierce both ends of four eggs with a pin. Then probe inside with a wider toothpick, put a straw to one hole and gently blow the egg contents into a bowl. Lay the empty egg shells on their side in a rectangle pattern and repeat the experiment. But first predict how many books will be held up this time.

TOP TIPS!

Ask an adult to help when you're cutting the shells.

REAL LIFE SCIENCE

Some of the most beautiful buildings in the world—the Taj Mahal, St. Paul's Cathedral, the US Capitol—have instantly recognizable domes. They look grand from the outside, but they also help create space inside. After all, with the dome doing the "heavy lifting," there's no need for lots of beams or columns to clutter up the space. For more than 1,300 years, the ancient Pantheon in Rome was the largest dome in the world until the Duomo was built in Florence.

Vinegar Vesuvius

The forces that build up beneath the Earth's surface can take hundreds or even thousands of years to break through and trigger a volcanic eruption. You needn't wait that long to produce a kitchen version, but you'll still need to stand back!

1

Add 3 cups (350 g) of flour, 1 cup (250 g) of salt, 1 cup (225 ml) of warm water and 2 tablespoons of cooking oil to the mixing bowl.

2

Mix those ingredients with the wooden spoon until the mixture is firm and smooth.

3

You will be shaping this mixture to form the slopes of the volcano. If it is too stiff, add a little more warm water.

4

Stand the bottle in the middle of the baking tray.

5

Spoon some of the flour mixture all around the base of the bottle.

6

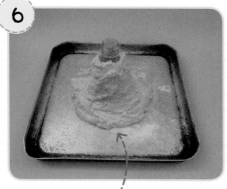

Add more mixture and shape it into a cone, surrounding (and hiding) the bottle. Make sure the top of the bottle doesn't get covered.

7

You now have the volcano as it would look before an eruption. It is much like a normal mountain but with a hole at the top.

8

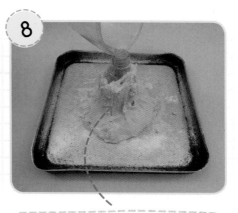

Fill the measuring cup with warm water and pour it carefully into the bottle until it's about two-thirds full.

9

Add a few drops of food coloring and 4 drops of dishwashing liquid to the bottle.

Add one tablespoon of baking soda to the mixture in the bottle.

10

11

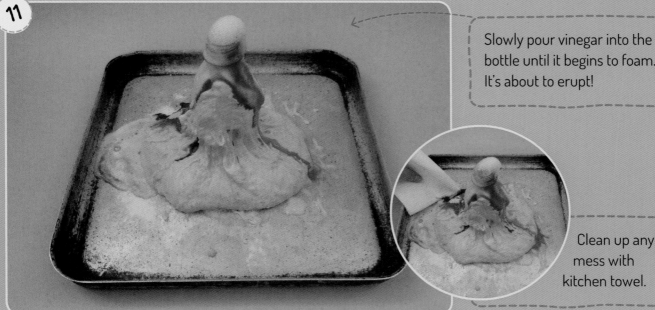

Slowly pour vinegar into the bottle until it begins to foam. It's about to erupt!

Clean up any mess with kitchen towel.

HOW DOES IT WORK?

You've done a good job of demonstrating how a real volcano erupts: gas builds up inside until it blows. The gas in your volcano was created by the reaction between the vinegar and the baking soda. They react to make carbon dioxide quickly.

Using warm water helped make the eruption more dramatic. That's because it increases the rate of the chemical reaction; scientists call that type of an ingredient a catalyst. The dishwashing liquid traps the gas bubbles, helping to form the "lava."

REAL LIFE SCIENCE

Some of the most powerful volcanic eruptions send lava, rocks, and ash high into the atmosphere. Scientists have observed volcanic ash more than 50 miles (80 km) above the Earth's surface.

TOP TIPS!

- Make sure you do this experiment by a sink or on a counter that you don't mind getting wet.

- It's a good idea to wear an apron throughout this experiment.

WHAT HAPPENS IF...?

Once the volcano has calmed down, you can trigger another eruption by adding a little more baking soda and then vinegar.

the Plant Maze

You've heard the expression "leading light," haven't you? In this experiment you'll see how light can lead a young plant through a simple maze. And you'll find that the plant really does follow the light... because it's hungry!

1 Place the playing card in the middle of one of the shorter ends of the shoebox and trace around it with the pencil.

2 Cut out the shape you just traced so that there's a hole in one end of the box.

3 Cut off the sides of the spare shoebox lid, so that you end up with just the top part, which is a large rectangle.

4 Measure the height (from the base to where it meets the lid) and also the width of the shoebox. Write down the measurements you've made.

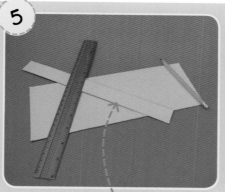

5 On the two shorter edges of the spare lid, mark a point that's the same as the "height" measurement you just made, then cut across from dot to dot.

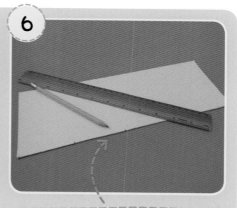

6 On the piece you've just cut, mark a point that's half of the "width" measurement you made earlier, then another the same distance along.

7

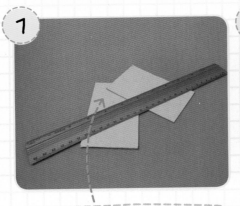

Cut across the spare lid at these two points. You should now have two pieces, each as high as the shoebox and half as wide.

8

Tape one of these pieces so that it stands upright—taped to the base and one of the long sides of the shoebox about one third of the way along.

9

Tape the second piece in the same way on the opposite side, about one third of the way farther along.

10

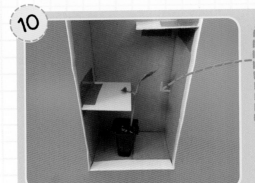

Stand the shoebox upright, with the cutout hole at the top, and put the plant at the bottom.

11

Put the lid back on and seal the edges completely with lots of tape. Then leave the box in a sunny location near a window.

12

After five days (or when the plant pokes through the hole), carefully remove the tape and open the lid. You'll see how the plant has zigzagged past the cutouts to reach the hole at the other end.

HOW DOES IT WORK?

This experiment shows phototropism at work. That big word comes from two Greek words meaning "light" (photo) and "movement" (tropism). And that's what plants do; they move toward a source of light. That's because they need light (plus water and warmth) to produce their own food.

The tips of plants contain a chemical called auxin, which helps the plant grow. Light destroys auxin, so the side of the plant that's in the light doesn't grow as much. But the other, shaded side keeps its auxin. It keeps growing, which bends the plant toward the source of light.

TOP TIPS!

You can transfer the bean plant to a larger pot or your yard and grow your own beans!

WHAT HAPPENS IF...?

Here's where you can make a scientific prediction. What will happen if you take the plant out of the shoebox and rest it on its own on a sunny windowsill?

REAL LIFE SCIENCE

What better plant to demonstrate phototropism than a sunflower? Or better yet, a field of sunflowers? The huge yellow flowers follow the course of the sun through the day, facing east in the morning, up at midday, and then finally west toward the setting sun.

Customized Celery

You've probably heard your parents say "drink up!" when you haven't finished your glass of water. But vegetables don't need to be asked—they drink up naturally. Here's an experiment to show you just how much, and how fast celery can "drink up."

YOU WILL NEED

- Celery stalk with leaves still attached
- Magnifying glass
- Blue food coloring
- Water
- Clear drinking glass
- Sharp knife
- Ruler

1

Half-fill the drinking glass with water and add 5 or 6 drops of food coloring. You want the water to turn dark blue.

2

Cut a 1 inch (3 cm) slice off the base of the celery (the "unleafy" end.)

3

Hold the celery stalk and look closely at the cut end through the magnifying glass. Observe the tubes that run up through it.

4

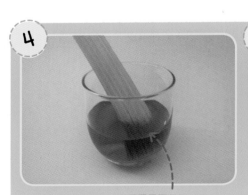

Rest the celery in the glass of water with the leafy side pointing up. Leave it there for four hours.

5

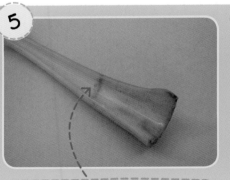

Take the celery out and check its color—it should have taken on a blueish tint. Even the leaves may be a little blue.

6

Cut the stalk into three or four 1 inch (3 cm) slices and use the magnifying glass to observe the tubes in each of them. See whether all of the tubes have changed color.

HOW DOES IT WORK?

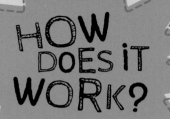

You've had a chance to see first-hand how plants absorb the water that they need to survive. Those tubes running up the stalk are called xylem. They transport water to all of the plant, much as you might sip a drink through a straw. You could see them at work by the way they—and other parts of the plant—changed color.

The xylem also carry essential nourishing minerals and chemicals that the plant's roots find in the soil. They get mixed in with the water just as the food dye formed a mixture with your water.

TOP TIPS!

Make sure you have an adult to do the cutting with the sharp knife.

WHAT HAPPENS IF...?

You can have real fun changing the color of white carnations. Try putting blue dye in one glass of water and red in another and then soak a carnation stem in each overnight. The next day add a "normal" white carnation to the others to make a "red, white, and blue" display.

REAL LIFE SCIENCE

Florists (people who sell flowers) use a version of this food-dye experiment to change the color of blossoms in the flowers they sell. One of the most popular orchids –"mystic blue"—gets its name from the dye that it absorbs.

A Matter of Taste

YOU WILL NEED

- Apple
- Pear (not too ripe – it should feel a bit like an apple)
- Sharp knife
- Vanilla extract
- 2 small plates
- Cotton balls
- 2 or 3 friends
- Blindfold (optional)

Question: When does an apple not taste like an apple? **Answer:** Only your nose knows! This simple experiment will have your friends wondering what's gone wrong with their taste buds. You'll all be surprised by how easy it is to trick your sense of taste.

1

Cut the apple and pear into about eight pieces each and set the pieces on the two plates. Make sure you know which plate has which fruit.

2

Get your friends to line up and close their eyes (or you could use a blindfold). Give each of them a slice of fruit. Ask them to taste it and identify it. They'll get it right—this time!

3

Put a few drops of vanilla extract onto cotton balls (one for each friend) and ask each of them to hold one of the cotton balls.

4

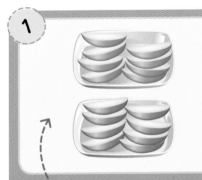

Now get them to hold the cotton ball under their nose and close their eyes.

Give them another piece of fruit while they are smelling the vanilla, and see how well they identify it. It's much harder now! Continue until you run out of fruit.

5

HOW DOES IT WORK?

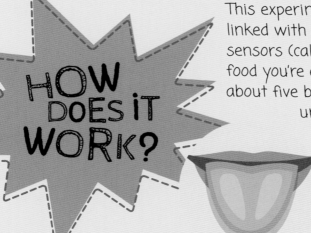

This experiment shows how closely the sense of taste is linked with the sense of smell. Your tongue has special sensors (called taste buds) to tell your brain about the food you're eating. But they can only pass on information about five basic tastes: sweet, sour, salty, bitter, and umami (a meaty flavour).

The rest of what you "taste" comes from what your nose picks up as smells. And in this case, the strong smell of vanilla overpowered the tastes of either fruit. Maybe that's why small children know to hold their nose when they have to eat vegetables!

TOP TIPS!

Make sure an adult uses the sharp knife to cut up the fruit.

REAL LIFE SCIENCE

There are many foods and drinks that smell wonderful but don't taste as good—or the other way around. Many people love the smell of fresh coffee but don't like the taste of the drink. And in parts of Asia, a fruit known as the durian can't be displayed in open-air markets because it smells so bad: but some people say that it tastes delicious.

WHAT HAPPENS IF...?

You can think up lots of ways to trick the taste buds. It works well if you sniff a strong-smelling food or liquid while eating something with less extreme taste. How about sniffing a raw onion while eating a stick of celery? You'll swear that you're eating the onion.

The Mummified Apple

Are you wondering what sort of spooky decoration you can prepare for a Halloween party? How about shrunken head? Not a real one, of course, but an apple that has undergone a scientific experiment. Don't go losing your head over it!

YOU WILL NEED

- Apple
- Apple corer
- Cereal bowl
- Salt
- Measuring jug
- Lemon juice
- Tablespoon
- Peeler
- Sharp knife
- Pen
- Baking pan
- Oven

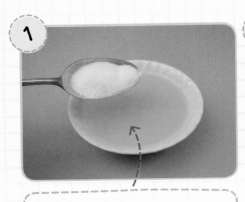

1. Mix one cup (225 ml) of lemon juice and one tablespoon of salt in the bowl.

2. Core the apple and carefully peel off the skin.

3. Roll the apple in the bowl of lemon juice and salt. Leave it for about a minute to give it a good soaking.

4. Draw eyes, nose, and a mouth on the apple and have an adult cut them out.

5. Roll the apple in the bowl again and then place it on a baking pan in an oven on a low heat, about 210°F (100°C.)

6. Keep it warming for 30 minutes or until the apple has dried out... to reveal a shrunken mummy face!

HOW DOES IT WORK?

You might not realize it but an apple—like many living things, both plant and animal—contains lots of water. And when water is warmed, as it is in the oven, it evaporates (turns into the gas called water vapor). Without all that water to hold it together and puff it out, the rest of the apple shrinks.

The lemon juice stops the apple flesh from turning brown. That process—when the surface of an object reacts with the oxygen in the air—is called oxidation. Here, the lemon juice prevented the air from reaching the flesh of the apple.

WHAT HAPPENS IF...?

You could try a similar experiment with another piece of fruit or vegetable to see whether it shrinks as much (or more) than the apple.

TOP TIPS!

It's best to have an adult use the corer, peeler and the oven.

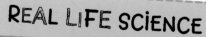
REAL LIFE SCIENCE

The bodies that ancient Egyptians preserved as mummies also shrank, for the same reason that your apple lost its size. The hot, dry air of Egypt acts like the warm oven in your experiment.

The Drooling Plant

YOU WILL NEED

- Healthy house plant
- 2 clear sandwich bags
- Clear tape
- Water

That sounds a bit disgusting, doesn't it? Would it be any better if this experiment had been called "plant pee"? Because it could have been. A lot goes into, and comes out from, plants all the time. You just need to know how to look.

1

Set a healthy house plant in a well-lit area, such as a sunny windowsill. Find a strong stem with a large leaf or—even better—a cluster of leaves.

2

Slide the sandwich bag over the leaf (or leaves) so that the mouth of the bag is close to the stem, and not crushing leaves.

3

Carefully secure the mouth of the bag with tape. You don't have to make it very tight— a little gap won't matter.

4

After two hours, remove the bag and examine it. You'll see drops of water lining the inside.

5

Repeat this experiment on the same leaves with a new bag, but water the plant well before you leave it. See whether the second bag collects more water.

116

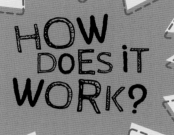

HOW DOES IT WORK?

This experiment is all about the way that plants can "suck" water up from the soil, all the way to the outermost leaves. Along the way, the plant is able to use useful minerals that are dissolved in the water. The process is called transpiration.

When it reaches the end of the line, the water evaporates from tiny holes in the leaves. But more water is being sucked in, so the process continues. And the rate sometimes increases if there's more water to be found. You might have found the same thing in the last step of this experiment, when you increased the water supply.

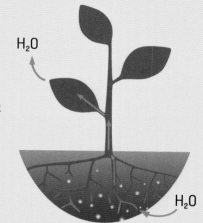

H_2O

H_2O

REAL LIFE SCIENCE

Not every plant can afford to lose water so easily. Plants in deserts, for example, can't waste precious water by letting it evaporate. That's why cactus plants and other desert-natives have such small leaves. The smaller the leaf, the less it allows water to escape through evaporation.

WHAT HAPPENS IF...?

You don't have to limit yourself to houseplants. Try "bagging" some low branches in trees. You could compare how much water each type of tree produces.

Trick Your Eyes

Have you ever dreamed of becoming a film director? Or an animator? You can become a bit of both with this "eye-catching" experiment. It's all about what your brain sees, and expects to see. OK: Lights... Camera... Action!

YOU WILL NEED

- Pack of sticky notes: 1 ½ x 2 inches (38 mm x 51 mm)
- Ball-point or fine marker pen

1 Lay the pack of notes on a table with the sticky end away from you.

2 Pressing down on the "sticky" end with a finger, bend the notes up toward you and let them go so that they flutter back. This is practice for later.

3 Draw a simple picture on the bottom page. Think of how the images in the picture might move during your movie.

4 On the next page up, draw a picture that's almost exactly the same, except for one part that's moved just a tiny bit. It might be someone's arm being raised or a bee zooming around.

5 Continue drawing a series of pictures, with just a bit of movement from page to page, until you reach the last page, which is at the top.

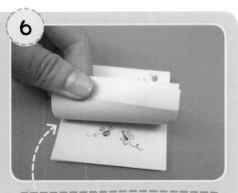

6 Repeat Step 2. But this time your movie will play out just like a cartoon on television.

HOW DOES IT WORK?

Believe it or not, you've been demonstrating the basic principles of filmmaking. You've also been revealing something very interesting about how your eyes (and brain) see moving things. Traditional film and animation work by showing a series of still images (like your drawings) very quickly.

Instead of seeing the images as jerky and awkward, your brain links them together into one seamless flow. That's because the images linger on the retina (in the back of the eye) and are still there when the next one arrives. The brain sees that as normal movement.

REAL LIFE SCIENCE

If you look at some of the very earliest silent films, the movement on screen is jerky. Cinema cameras soon developed to shoot film images at 16 frames (still images) per second, which made movement look much smoother. Later cameras increased this to 24 frames per second. Modern cameras push things even higher, some as much as 60 frames per second.

WHAT HAPPENS IF...?

You can test this idea of images lingering on the eye (also called "persistence of vision") by changing how fast you flip the pages in your flip-book movie. You should find that it seems more realistic if you flip faster.

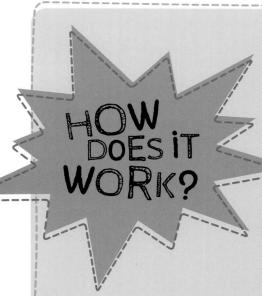

The Cress Race

YOU WILL NEED

- 3 teacups
- Water
- Packet of cress seeds
- Teaspoon
- Cotton balls

When scientists conduct experiments, they use "variables"—things that are different in the objects they're observing. In this experiment, you're examining two variables—light and water. Plants need both, don't they? Observe and decide.

1

Put three cotton balls at the base of each teacup.

2

Sprinkle 1 teaspoon of cress seeds into each cup, resting on the cotton.

3

Pour enough water to dampen the cotton in two of the cups, but don't add water to the third.

4

Put the "dry" cup and one of the dampened-cotton cups on a sunny windowsill, and the third cup should go in a dark cupboard.

5

Monitor the cups for five days, adding a little water to the "dampened" cups if they start to dry out.

6

Compare the growth of the cress in all three cups. The cress in the cup that had light and water should have grown the most.

HOW DOES IT WORK?

Most of us know that plants need light and water in order to produce their own food so they can grow and remain healthy. It won't come as a surprise that the cress that had both light and water did the best. And the seeds that had no water didn't change at all.

What might surprise you is how tall the cress grew in the dark. That's because they were trying to find light (to produce food). It also explains why they were so yellow: plants produce chlorophyll (a green coloring) when they have enough light and water to make their own food.

WHAT HAPPENS IF...?

There's another variable that determines how much plants can grow: heat. All three of your teacups had enough heat, but if you want to see how important it is, try another experiment. Compare your "light and water" cress teacup with an identical one that's been kept outside in cold weather. You should see that the warmer conditions on the windowsill helped the cress grow more.

TOP TIPS!

- It would be a good idea to label the cups, so that you don't mix them up.
- Don't use your mom's favorite cup!

REAL LIFE SCIENCE

Although plants need water, light, and warmth to grow and remain healthy, they don't all need the same amounts of these variables. Think of how little water a cactus needs, or how flowers can still grow in some of the coldest places.

Plant Breath

We all know that plants need water, sunlight, and some gases (especially carbon dioxide) from the air to produce food. And that they get rid of oxygen as waste. But wouldn't it be fun to witness this process as it happens? Here's how you can.

1

Make sure you've chosen leaves of about the same size. Test each to make sure it will fit across the glass without needing to be bent.

2

Fill both glasses almost to the top with water and rest a leaf on the water of each glass.

3

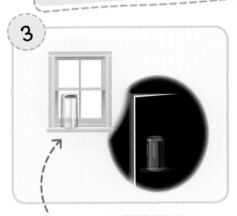

Place one glass on a sunny windowsill and the other in a dark place like a closet or cupboard.

4

Wait one hour and then compare both glasses. Look for bubbles on the edge of the leaves and on the glasses themselves. Try looking even more closely with a magnifying glass to see the tiniest bubbles.

5

Return the glasses to the windowsill and dark area for another hour. See whether there are more bubbles.

HOW DOES IT WORK?

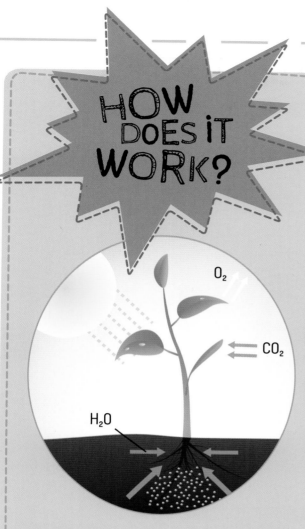

O_2

CO_2

H_2O

The bubbles you observed were oxygen, the waste given off by plants after they have created their own food through a process called photosynthesis. That long word comes from two Greek words, photo (meaning "light") and synthesis (meaning "making"). And that's exactly what plants do: they make food from light.

Because plants need light to make food, the leaf kept in the dark wasn't able to make much food. How do we know? Because making more food would mean producing more waste. And there was lots more of that waste—the bubbles of oxygen—in the glass that was in the sunny spot.

REAL LIFE SCIENCE

You can sometimes see a difference in leaves on the same tree. Those nearest the top of the tree—with more exposure to light—usually look greener and healthier than those below (shaded from the direct light). You'd probably see more oxygen bubbles coming from those higher leaves for the same reason.

WHAT HAPPENS IF...?

If you picked a leaf and left it in the sun for an hour before placing it in water, you'd see very few bubbles. Probably none, because the leaf would have died. The water is important not just in making food, but in helping the food spread within a plant.

123

Burp in a Bag

Is this really an experiment about burping? Yes, although it's not you who's doing the burping. But it is a living organism—a tiny relative of mushrooms that we call yeast. In fact, you probably eat the results of those burps every day, and enjoy it!

YOU WILL NEED

- Dry yeast
- Warm water (from faucet is fine: about the temperature of bathwater)
- Cold water
- Teaspoon
- White sugar
- 3 sealable sandwich bags

1

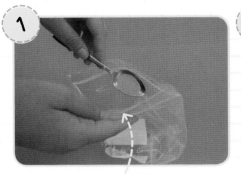

Add one teaspoon of dry yeast to each bag.

2

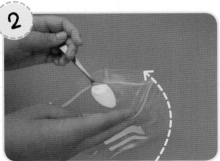

Add one teaspoon of sugar to the second and third bags.

3

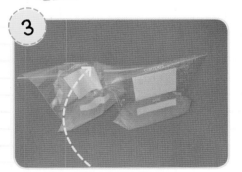

Add 1 inch (3 cm) of cold water to the first and second bags and seal them. You might want to label them.

4

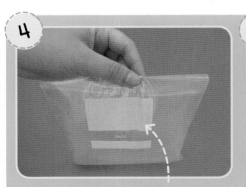

Add 1 inch (3 cm) of warm water to the third bag and seal it.

5

Line up all three bags along a sunny windowsill. Make sure you still know which is which!

6

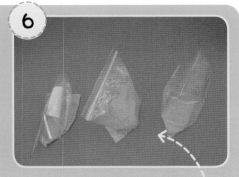

After 20 minutes, observe the bags. The first will hardly have changed, the second will have some suds inside and have puffed up a bit. But the third (with sugar and warm water) will have changed the most.

HOW DOES IT WORK?

Yeast really is a living organism and like you (another living organism) it sometimes produces gas when it eats. The dry yeast in packets is alive, but only becomes active when it has something to eat (the sugar). It feeds on the sugar and produces a gas (carbon dioxide) as waste. That's what the yeast "burped" and what filled up the sandwich bag.

But this experiment tells us a little more. Like many small organisms, yeast prefers a certain temperature. In its case, that temperature is about the same as the temperature of your bath. And that's why the third bag filled up the most: it had its food (the sugar) and the ideal temperature.

TOP TIPS!

Make sure the water isn't too hot—"warm to the touch" is a good description of bathwater temperature.

WHAT HAPPENS IF...?

You can recreate the success of "bag number 3" by mixing the warm water, yeast, and sugar in a small soda bottle and then sliding a balloon over the mouth. The carbon dioxide will start to blow up the balloon.

REAL LIFE SCIENCE

What was that about "eating the result of burps"? Yeast is a key ingredient in most breads. Think of all those holes in the bread you eat. Those are the spaces where yeast bubbled up in the bread dough before it was baked. When bakers talk about bread dough "rising," they're describing how the yeast bubbles and fluffs up the bread. Without it, the loaf would be solid.

The Bouncing Egg

Fried eggs, poached eggs, and scrambled eggs are all tasty, but would you ever order a bouncing egg for breakfast? It might not be your first choice, but it's a lot more fun to play with. Just don't eat the results of this crazy recipe!

YOU WILL NEED

- An egg (uncooked)
- Vinegar
- Old drinking glass, at least "2 eggs high" inside
- Paper towel
- Spoon

1

Tilt the glass and carefully put the egg inside it.

2

Stand the glass upright and pour in enough vinegar to cover the egg completely. You'll start to see some bubbles emerging from the shell.

3

Leave the egg in the glass for four days, but observe it regularly to note changes in the shell. The bubbling will stop when the shell has dissolved.

4
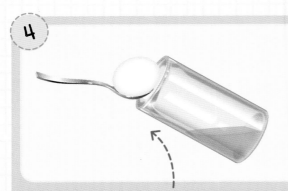

Tilt the glass a little over a basin and gently remove the egg, using the spoon. Lay the egg on two pieces of paper towel to let the vinegar drain off its surface. The shell will have disappeared, replaced with a waxy coating.

5

You can hold the egg carefully and it won't burst, so try dropping it from a low height, about 2 inches (5 cm). See how high you can go before things get very messy!

126

HOW DOES IT WORK?

You've just used a chemical reaction to work a little magic. Eggshells contain calcium, a chemical element that gives them their hardness. Your bones are hard because they also have lots of calcium.

Vinegar contains a substance called acetic acid, which reacts with the calcium of the eggshell. That reaction produces the gas called carbon dioxide (those were the bubbles), and it uses up the calcium along the way. What's left is called the egg membrane, the almost transparent and flexible covering of the egg.

REAL LIFE SCIENCE

Many rocks in the ground are made up of calcium carbonate, the same as eggshells. As rain seeps through the rock, the calcium carbonate is dissolved. That's because the water contains small amounts of acid. Sometimes the water reaches a cave, and the air in the cave reverses the process. The calcium carbonate reappears as towering stalactites and stalagmites.

WHAT HAPPENS IF...?

Try putting the "shell-less egg" in another glass, then cover it with water and put it in the refrigerator for 24 hours. It will have become much bigger. That's because the soft membrane allows water to pass through it, "pumping up" the inside of the egg.

TOP TIPS!

Make sure that you test the egg somewhere that you can clean up easily.

Glossary

air pressure The constant pressing of air on everything it touches.

amplify To make larger or greater.

buoyancy The ability of an object to float or rise in a liquid or gas.

catapult An ancient weapon for throwing heavy rocks or other objects.

center of mass The point that has the mass of an object evenly distributed around it; also called the center of gravity or balancing point.

chlorophyll A green substance that lets plants create food from carbon dioxide and water.

circuit The closed path that an electrical current follows.

conduct To transmit heat or electricity.

density The amount of mass something has in relation to its volume (or space that it takes up).

electrolyte A substance that increases the ability of a liquid to carry an electrical charge.

electron A negatively charged particle that forms part of an atom.

element A substance that cannot be broken down into other substances using chemistry.

energy The power or ability to do work such as moving. Energy can be transferred from one object to another, but it cannot be destroyed.

force The strength of a particular energy at work.

frequency How often something occurs.

friction The force that causes a moving object to slow down.

fulcrum The support that balances a lever when it is working.

gravity The force that causes all objects to be attracted to each other.

ignite To catch fire or begin to burn.

insulation Material that prevents or slows the transfer of energy from one object to another.

kinetic energy The energy of movement.

lava Hot, melted rock that erupts from a volcano.

lever A simple machine for lifting which consists of a rigid beam pivoting on a hinge called a fulcrum.

lubricant A material, often liquid, that reduces friction.

magnetism A force, related to electrical currents, that creates an attraction between certain materials.

mass A measure of how much matter something contains.

molecule The smallest unit of a substance, such as oxygen, that has all the properties of that substance.

phototropism The movement of plant parts towards the source of light.

photosynthesis The process that allows plants to use sunlight to change water and carbon dioxide into food for itself.

polymer A large molecule made up of many repeated smaller units.

potential energy The energy that is stored in an object, based on the object's position; a ball at the top of a hill has potential energy that can be converted to kinetic energy.

primary colors Groups of three basic colors, which can be combined to make a much wider range of colors.

prism A clear, solid object that refracts light as it passes through so that it is broken up into the colors of the rainbow.

proton A positively charged particle that forms part of an atom.

radiation Waves of energy sent out by sources of light or heat.

refract To cause waves (of light, heat, or sound) to bend as they pass through a different material.

sound A vibration that passes through air, water, or other materials and which the ear converts to recognizable impulses.

static electricity Electricity that is held or discharged (sent off) by an object.

surface tension A force that binds molecules on the outer layer of a liquid together.

vacuum A space containing no matter.

xylem Plant tissue that transports water and minerals from the roots up to all the other parts of the plant.